ENDORSEMENTS

"I found myself time and time again being drawn in by Joel's stories. I walked through the jungles of Vietnam and even started to feel ants crawling on me. But the most pleasant surprises always came after the stories. Instead of continuing in the jungle, like a clearing in the forest, Abide in Me reveals the love of God. It emerges like a camouflaged figure that has been standing beside you the whole time."

Kevin Weatherby
Pastor and Founder of Save the Cowboy

"If it were not for Joel's early detection radar concerning my PTSD leading me to get help at the Veterans Administration and take AIM, I may not be here today. Thanks for the lifeline and transparency in this book-"

George Kirsten
Pastor, West Bowles Community Church
Former Navy combat search and rescue helicopter pilot,
Vietnam (1968–1971)

"This book is about Joel Trenkle's life. Not all of his life, but about key events which formed him and left his heart very damaged. These included being publically put down by his second-grade schoolteacher and becoming the laughingstock of the school. Joel began acting out, because he was dyslectic and could not learn. Joel became the problem student, because he could not find a place to fit in. Finally, Joel went to Vietnam and came back in even worse condition than when he had left. Now he had Post Traumatic Stress Sy

wrecked. He became an alcoholic, lived alone, was totally destitute, and was right on the verge of taking his own life.

"Yet today he is healed, and Joel functions as an effective minister of the gospel of our Lord and Savior, Jesus Christ. How did this happen? Well, Joel tells his story in the most interesting way. You will be captivated by it and drawn in, and you too will discover the grace of God that heals the wounds in man's heart.

"The path toward healing involved Scripture, the voice of God, forgiveness, deliverance, inner healing, repentance for sinful thoughts and behaviors, and finding that a broken life can be restored!
"As you read this book, you will discover hope springing up in your heart. You will see that no matter where you are at, Jesus is reaching out to take you by the hand, to touch you, and to heal you.

Let Joel share with you the steps the Lord took him through. Find wholeness. Find Jesus. Be restored to all that God intended you to be."

"Joel received his Doctorate from the school which I am the president of, Christian Leadership University. We are so proud of him and of his accomplishments."

Dr. Mark Virkler
A friend and child of the King

ABIDE IN ME

Abide in Me

AIM

Dr. Joel N. Trenkle and Doni L. Trenkle

WestBow
PRESS
A DIVISION OF THOMAS NELSON

ISBN: 978-1-4497-4981-1 (e)
ISBN: 978-1-4497-4980-4 (sc)
ISBN: 978-1-4497-4979-8 (hc)

Library of Congress Control Number: 2012907896

WestBow Press books may be ordered through booksellers or by contacting:

WestBow Press
A Division of Thomas Nelson
1663 Liberty Drive
Bloomington, IN 47403
www.westbowpress.com
1-(866) 928-1240

Unless otherwise noted, scripture verses are taken from The Complete Jewish Bible: David H. Stern, Complete Jewish Bible (Clarksville, Maryland: Jewish New Testament Publications, Inc., 1998).

Cover Design by Steven Hegarty

Printed in the United States of America

WestBow Press rev. date: 5/10/2012

CONTENTS

PREFACE

Although this book contains many stories about my own life, it is not about me. It is about God's love and forgiveness. The stories demonstrate how a person can turn—and be turned—180 degrees from the path he was created to walk and find his way back. There are some necessary ingredients for this action to take place, which are demonstrated and can be learned in this book.

First, we must have faith in God—faith that He loves us and wants to have an everlasting relationship with us. This is not always easy, given that many of us feel abandoned by Him or do not feel He has ever been active in our lives.

Second, we must realize that God has an enemy. As His sons and daughters, so do we. The evil and calamity in our lives are not from God. We have to get to a point where we can look honestly at our own actions and take responsibility for our own mistakes and willful sin. None of us want to admit that we have deliberately lived lives of self-gratification at the expense of others and ourselves. This step, although the most difficult, is the one that will give our Lord Jesus the ability to begin to work in us.

Third, we must accept the help of our Lord. He will direct and guide us to a place of forgiveness, wholeness, and peace through the power of the Holy Spirit of God, who lives in each person who believes in Him. We can and must learn to listen for the voice of God.

Last, we must learn to take captive the thoughts that are intended to take us back to a place of familiarity—that place where the self reigns instead of our Lord Jesus. It might seem unbelievable, but many people will choose to remain in a painful, destructive lifestyle that they have known rather than embrace a new life where they release their will to God. This is because they have been fooled into believing that they have control. Like anything else in this life, letting God sit in the driver's seat requires patience and hard work. It will not all happen at one time. It is a learned behavior—one that took me over forty years to realize and put into daily (even hourly) practice.

I am certain if you read and work through this book, your life will be changed, and your relationships with others will improve. Most important, you will enjoy your new relationship with your Savior.

ACKNOWLEDGMENTS

I need to thank my Savior, Jesus, for setting me free from the chains that held me captive for most of my life. I thank my wife and co-author for her willingness to persevere and my children for enduring many years of my control. I would like to thank my father-in-law, Dewayne Neufeld, for his role in showing me how a godly man lives and most of all for how he prays for his family, friends, and loved ones. I would like to thank Dr. Randy Lumpp from Regis University for his belief in me. I would also like to thank Dr. Mark Virkler, president and founder of Christian Leadership University, for his obedience to our Lord in listening to and teaching others to directly hear the voice of God.

CHAPTER ONE

Abiding in Changing Times

The purpose of this book is to give direction during times of difficulty and uncertainty—times just like the ones we are living in now. Our past is gone, and it can no longer predict what the future will be. There was a time, just a few years ago, when an education in a particular field could ensure the probability of a good future, but that is no longer true. Often by the time a student earns a degree in a given field, what he has just learned is obsolete. We are living in a period like none other in the history of humankind. Evil seems to have the freedom to express itself in every area of life, while the attempts of righteous people are thwarted and even condemned.

Dr. Charles R. Swindoll, in his co-authored book *The Road to Armageddon,*[1] states that he was surprised when one of his grandchildren, a sixth-grade student in California, recently told him "they decided that we have to walk through metal detectors now to come to school." Dr. Swindoll goes on to talk about the problems teachers faced in 1940 from students, quoting from Steven Covey, in his book *The Seven Habits of Highly Effective Families,*[2] "They were talking out of turn, chewing gum, making noise, running in the halls, cutting in line, daily dress code infractions, and littering. Contrast this with the problems in our schools in the 1990s! They were drug abuse, alcohol abuse, pregnancy, suicide, rape, robbery, and assault."

To compound the unchecked rise of evil, in most of our public schools, our youth are being subjected to the mind- and soul-altering effects of what is called "political correctness." This is like sugar added to poisoned Kool-Aid to cover the bitter taste. This cup they are drinking contains the lies of the world, which condones such things as abortion, socialism, and same-sex marriage and even promotes the acceptance of religions that are completely evil in their beliefs and practices. To reject or speak out against some of them can now be a violation of law. We are told we should learn to coexist with them. These concepts have now been taught in our schools for three generations. We have parents who were raised in this new culture teaching their children that this is the way, the truth, and the life. To teach or speak the real truth is now called bigotry or prejudice.

Our adversary, the Devil, has been working hard to plant this acceptance of evil in our minds, minimizing the potency of this drink so we will accept it as a norm. The moral beliefs and behaviors that were a guide to previous generations in this country had roots in sound biblical principles. Today we are pulled further away from the Scriptures and the directions found in them. We allow the truth to be condemned. It would seem we are slipping into a culture where the Bible—the very Word spoken by God—is no longer relevant. These biblical values are considered confining and condemning by today's lifestyles. *What is wrong will seem right, and the righteous will be persecuted for the truth.*

How did we get so far away from the great command of our Lord, "go into all nations and preach the Good News" (Mark 16:15)? This passage in Scripture can find no relevance in a literal coexistence. Within the concept of coexistence, there is no need to preach the good news, because we have become complacent toward the world and simply accept every religion and lifestyle. The good news of Jesus Christ teaches us that through His blood, shed for our sinfulness, we can now be free of an ungodly life. This truly is good news! We have

> Within the concept of coexistence, there is no need to preach the good news, because we have become complacent toward the world and simply accept every religion and lifestyle.

been given a command to bring this good news to the lost; this is not always an easy task. Our precious Lord told us, "They hated Me, know that they will hate you also." And again, He stated, "You will be persecuted for following Me" (Matthew 24:9).[4] If we run in fear at the thought of being persecuted and continue to listen to man instead of the good news of our Lord, we will fail at this task. We will abandon our God and gratify ourselves, drinking the cup of Kool-Aid that can produce only death.

Grandparents and parents have a duty to give our children direction and hope in a fast-changing world. We cannot give this direction based on worldly standards, for the standard of this world has become ungodly. It is our responsibility, especially in view of the fact that the collapse of moral values has occurred during our watch. Since the end of World War II, we have been in pursuit of what pleasures we could glean from worldly endeavors. As a result, this generation of parents does not know the truth outlined by our Lord in order to pass it on to its children.

For a very long time, people have taken their eyes off our precious Lord and focused instead on the world and its successes. We've fallen prey to concepts like climbing the corporate ladder and letting professional educators teach our children, because they can do a better job. We've left godly values to follow the American dream. Where is that dream now? We have paid a very high price for something that has become a nightmare. Sadly, man has been preaching a dream focused on success in this world instead of the dream of a future and eternity with God Almighty.

The good news is that there is still good news. If we know the truth, we can speak it out and set the captives free. We can give our children and grandchildren real hope by opening the Scriptures and reading the promises in them—the same promises that our ancestors found to be true when they abided in Christ. There is hope, and it is found in the real, living way, truth, and life—Jesus, our Lord.

This hope for our eternal future and the realization of the promises of God do not just happen. Our Lord Jesus tells us we must *desire* to have a relationship with Him. "Seek and you will find; Knock and the door will be opened to you!"[5] Even when Jesus was on earth, people did not seek Him for relationships, but rather for what He could do for them. Some desired to make Him king; others just wanted Him to perform a miracle for them. Very few wanted to find salvation, and in the end, there was only one disciple standing at the foot of His cross. What our Lord desires is to have all of His children come to Him and lay their heads on His chest as John did at the Last Supper, believing and placing their faith in Him. This leads to an abiding life in Christ! The richness and fullness of life that He offers can be found when you seek Him. It is not a guarantee that life will be trouble-free. God's Word tells us that we will have troubles, but Jesus will see to it that our burdens will be light and easy to carry, because He will be there (John 16:33).

In Acts 9:16, before Hananyah went to heal Sha'ul (Paul), the Lord told Hananyah that He would show Paul how much he would suffer on account of Jesus' name.[7] Yet Paul was willing to take up that cross and follow Him. He was willing to do the work that our Lord set out for him. This was because Paul abided in Christ. He rested in our Lord. He had a clear vision of his heavenly reward. It does not matter what a person does for a living; there will be trouble in it. If we believe in Jesus and abide in Him, our strength won't fail. We are not promised an easy life but that our names will be written in the book of life. John 14:6 says, "I am the way the truth and the life he who believes in Me even though he shall die will live."

Chapter Meditation

Before you continue with this book, please take a moment to write your personal thoughts regarding your life. You might talk about your childhood dreams and expectations. Goals you reached, or did not reach and why. Spiritually, what is your relationship with the Father?

CHAPTER TWO

Comfort in Your Closet

In the Gospel of Matthew, verses 28-30, Jesus tells us "Come to Me all you who are weary and burdened, and I will give you rest. Take My yoke upon you and learn from Me, for I am gentle and humble of heart, and you will find rest for your souls. For My yoke is easy and My burden is light." (New International Version) Believers in Jesus who learn to truly abide in Him find that their yokes really are easier, and their burdens do seem lighter. These were the promises of our Lord, and they are true. Do we have problems? Yes! Do some of us experience sickness, death, poverty, and hardships? Again, the answer is yes! If you are presently in one of these situations, you are probably thinking something like, *Sure, this is easy for you to say! Show me, and I will believe.* Well, the apostle Thomas said the same thing, and so did I a few years ago. What I am asking is that you take the fact that Jesus will help you if you believe in Him on faith for now.

I am pretty sure that by the end of this book, you will be able to put your trust in God, but the questions still remain: *Why should we abide in Him? What is the benefit?* I feel I can best answer these and other questions by using my own life as an example. I feel certain many folks can relate to the life-threatening and life-altering experiences I have lived through, all of which have come together to help me to abide in our Lord.

> Learning is specific to our individual uniqueness; therefore, the style of teaching needs to be uniquely and individually directed.

To reach a place in life where one is willing to trust in our Lord and abide in Him is different for each person, because each person's life and environment is individually unique. Therefore, the road to this abiding rest and comfort is individually specific. For me, this journey began when I was very young. Although I was not always cognizant of the fact that our Lord was always with me, as I look back, it is clear He was most certainly there.

Have you ever had trouble learning or staying on task? Do you know someone who does? I have been blessed with what today is known as attention deficit disorder with hyperactivity (ADHD). I discovered I am also dyslexic. I did not realize this until about 1983, when I was required to go through a battery of psychiatric testing for a pastoral care and counseling degree. The psychologist who was conducting the tests seemed surprised that I did not already know about these traits, but they did explain some issues around my many early academic challenges.

As a child, I was told that I was both stupid and a troublemaker. I have to plead guilty to the troublemaker part! I did my best to live *down* to these expectations. I do not believe any child is stupid. Learning is specific to our individual uniqueness; therefore, the style of teaching needs to be uniquely and individually directed. This is not always possible in our schools with more than thirty students in each classroom. All this is the backdrop to a stage that was set for an extremely depressing childhood, which—but for the grace of God—would have ended in a life of failure.

I am the third child in a family of four children. In the 1940s and early '50s, there was very little, if any, knowledge of my disorders or how to treat them. My older two brothers excelled in everything. My oldest brother pulled straight A's in academics and girls. My next-oldest brother, also an A student, received many letters and awards in football and track. Then there was me. The same teachers who taught my older brothers could not understand why I was so impossible. I was always in some sort of trouble for talking in class or daydreaming. When called upon to answer a question, I rarely even knew where we were within the topic we were studying. Actually, I am fairly certain I was only called out so the teacher could blast me from my personal bubble back into the classroom. The teachers knew I would probably not have the answer. When it came time to do homework well, I found many more important discoveries in my own imaginative mind, and I'm afraid that did not leave much time for homework.

At the end of World War II, there was a great deal of government propaganda attempting to lead people to believe that life was going to be completely changed for the better. Parents were told that their children would have college degrees, and everyone would own a home in suburbia. I can recall quite clearly my second-grade teacher asking each student to tell the rest of the class what he or she expected to do for a living. With great anticipation of the future, each of my classmates talked about their aspirations to become doctors, lawyers, scientists, and engineers. I told them I wanted to be a truck driver. I thought driving a truck would be a wonderful way to see the country and let someone else pay for the gas. Actually, my desire to drive a truck was most likely due to my personal dream of getting out of Denver and the life I was living. Well, the class erupted in laughter as the teacher exclaimed, "A truck driver? Don't you know they have to load and unload those big things by themselves every day?" Apparently driving a truck did not present a picture of a successful career. For the rest of that year, every time a student did not do well on a test or didn't turn in a homework assignment, the teacher would remark, "Do you want to grow up to be a dumb truck driver like Trenkle?"

By the end of that year, I had no self-esteem left. I had no support from my family members, who could not understand why I couldn't just be like my brothers. The kids I went to school with did not want to be seen with me, and by the age of seven or eight, I was depressed and actively suicidal. I remember sitting on the floor of my closet, enjoying the darkness as I closed the world out, believing I had been adopted into my family and wishing with all my heart that I could just die. I imagined how I could hang myself from my closet rod, but after my first attempt, I discovered two facts: first, the rod could not support my weight, and second, hanging really hurt! I also knew that if I tried and failed (failure having been the history of my young life), I would only have to tell another lie in order to cover the truth of my own despair.

Flash forward a few years—actually, a lifetime. While completing my doctoral degree at Christian Leadership University, I took a course titled "Prayers that Heal the Heart." Through this course, I finally presented these things to our Lord in prayer. I asked Him, "Where were you in my painful childhood?"

This is what I heard: "Joel, I have been calling you from your youth. When you had no one else to abide in—no one else to hold and comfort you as you sat on your closet floor—I was with you. I sat with you and held you as you wept tears of loneliness. When you cried out to Me, I was with you—even though you did not know it. I am in each person's closet, waiting to comfort him or her. I knitted each person in his or her mother's womb. Would I ever stop loving my creation?"

I replied, "Lord, you would continue, because you could do nothing else."

The love Jesus has for us is immeasurable. Sometimes it is not immediately apparent. Our love for Him and our faith in Him must be nurtured and developed as we move through the trials of life. This very personal relationship with Him begins with the basic beliefs of the Christian faith—that Jesus came to earth, died for our sins, and rose again so we could be with Him. However, the one who created us, loves us, and died for us knows that we cannot, by our own strength, remain in Him. Simply having knowledge of His life and death isn't enough to keep us on the path to righteousness. We need more than this; we need Him, and we need His Spirit! Through Jesus' death, we were purchased from a second eternal death. When we acknowledge this through baptism and receive the Holy Spirit, we have the start of an abundant life.

The Spirit of God is our map to this abundant life; without Him, we cannot be sure where we are going. The Holy Spirit directs our paths, speaks to our hearts, and lets us know when our thoughts, actions, and directions are not right—when we are not abiding in Him. Without God's Spirit, we fall back into human lusts and desires and lose our way. With Him, the kingdom of God is always within us. The Spirit gives us strength to continually check our hearts and discern the presence of the Lord before we make a decision or statement. What we do and say should be pleasing to God. These are the first steps to abiding with Him.

God created us for this relationship—this abiding. He created us to have communion with Him, and He longs to be with us. He is jealous for us. I believe it has always been His desire to abide with us; that is why we were created. Remember the story of my childhood—the little boy in the closet? I did not realize at the time how much God loved me. I did not realize anyone loved me, but *the Creator of the universe sat on that closet floor with me*. He was there, because when I was a child, He chose to love me and abide with me! God chooses to love all of us, regardless of what we think of ourselves. He desired this love relationship with man from the very beginning. God created the first man and woman for companionship, love, and fellowship. They enjoyed an unbroken bond with their Creator until what He gave them was not enough and they desired more. Their abiding relationship with a loving God was shattered when they disobeyed His perfect will for them.

Adam and Eve's sin against God opened the door for all mankind to see the truth of good and evil. Instead of walking in the garden in the cool of the evening with the one who loves us passionately, discussing the events of the day, we are forced to weigh every thought, word, and deed and then choose right from wrong, good or evil. We are in a constant battle for peace, choosing between self-serving desire and God's plan for our lives. Our Lord desires a relationship with us; this is why He suffered and died. That is how great His love is—but His love is not the issue. Do we desire a relationship in which we are totally consumed by Him? Do we desire to abide with Him? Does man desire a relationship with God over the pleasure he sees here on earth—over his personal agenda? Adam and Eve were not content with their relationship with the Father. They wanted to be as the Father is. The moment they took their eyes off the garden, they began to lust for more than what they had.

When we take our eyes off the Lord and the precious gifts that we have been given, we open ourselves up to the adversary. The necessities of life are natural requests, but we are to ask the Father with the expectation that he knows our needs and what is best for us—what we can handle now and in the times to come. Learning to be at peace with what we have and trusting Him for the future are a huge part of abiding in Christ.

The apostles learned these lessons of abiding and trusting and shared them with us in the Scriptures. They had their own desires and expectations of Jesus, even after living with Him for over three years. The apostles learned the truth and depth of their relationship with our Lord by losing Him. Jesus taught them to abide with Him and the Father through the Holy Spirit and love their neighbors. All the while, they had their eyes focused on accomplishing mighty works on earth through His miraculous powers. Once He was in the grave, their desire to make Him an earthly king (Matthew 16:22–23) so they would be free of Roman oppression became meaningless. Just like Adam and Eve, they were faced with the emptiness of life without God's presence. This is true today as well. When our desire is for the here and now, we give up the right to live in His presence and walk with Him in the cool of the evening.

James 4:4 tells us that we cannot be a friend to the world without being an enemy of God. Adam and Eve took their eyes off the Father—

off of what was real and tangible—and pursued a dream. That dream was not from the Father; it was from the enemy, and it was not real. They turned from the real to the false—from a truth to a lie. They wanted the lie to be real, not fully understanding why the Father did not want them to see or experience the depth of the reality between good and evil. The apostles witnessed everything Jesus did and said, but they did so through their own filters of personal desire and prophetic expectation. If we are to abide in Him, then our focus should always be on things that are good, lovely, and pure—on things that are eternal.

Today, the difference between good and evil is pretty evident, isn't it? Well, maybe not. When news reports showing people blown up in airports or buses by a terrorist, the evil is apparent. This black-or-white difference may become gray however, when it comes to telling the truth or a lie. That lie could be just as destructive, to another person, as the terrorist bomb. Our choices center on our personal desires. Do you desire to abide in Jesus, trust in Him, and rest in His arms? Do you desire to please and serve the Almighty God or to gratify the self? Desire is a matter of the heart—that is why our Lord says He will judge a person's heart! Out of the heart and mouth of man come either good or evil (Matthew 15:18–19).

If a person's desire is to return to the garden—to attend to things the Father gave and be content with His blessings —then the service to the Father is clear. If a person is not content with what the Father chooses to give him or her, then the desire to forsake God gives rise to sin. This discontent begins with the desire to have more, and since this desire does not come from above, the doorway of destruction is opened for us to walk through. We are shown what we don't have, and our lust drives us forward—away from abiding—toward a long hallway, which becomes more difficult to walk and darkens with each step. Soon we will not see clearly and lose our direction. Worldly pleasures will not bring satisfaction if they are not from the Father. They are deceptive!

Because we are created in the likeness and image of God, we have within us a natural desire to be united with Him—to abide with

Him. If we remain in this darkness, desires will present themselves, and there will be new and different thrills to seek. This entire journey into darkness is designed to cause people to lose their inner hunger for unity with God. We begin to desire things that are created instead of the Creator. The Father's desire is that we look like Him in our actions, think like Him, love like Him, and be one with Him. His desire is to abide in us! It is His desire that we leave the darkness of our individual closets and enter into His light, visions, and dreams for an amazing life in Him. Abide in Him!

<u>Chapter Meditations</u>

1. Are you happy and content with your life?

2. Do you want more than you have been given?

3. If you were given the opportunity to open a door and walk into the kingdom of God, would you open it and walk through?

4. Is there some part of your life that you feel you could not lay down and walk away from?

CHAPTER THREE

Sister Mary Elvadine

Many believers in Jesus only feel connected with Him during the once-a-week trip to their places of worship. I have a dear friend who quips that because he goes to confession on Saturday and receives Communion on Sunday, he hopes he dies on Monday, because by the time Friday rolls around, he always feels his salvation is questionable. Although this is a little humorous, it does seem that many live their lives with no greater expectation than this. The truth is that this is not what our Lord directed us to do. From the time He began His ministry until now, He has always demonstrated that His desire is to have the kind of relationship that becomes a lifestyle for us. This lifestyle happens through forgiveness and grace, not a once-a-week trip to a building. I learned my first lesson about forgiveness and grace in the sixth grade.

As you recall from the last chapter, I was blessed with ADHD. Because of this, from about the second grade on, my assigned seating was always the front desk in the center row—in front of the teacher's desk. Whenever we went outside for recess, my assigned place was first in line—right next to the teacher. I neglected to mention that the school I attended was a parochial school, taught by nuns. They all wore black gowns that draped to the floor, complemented by black veils with white hoods that stuck out in front like small baseball hats. These seemed to be held on by white wraps that came down under the chin. The nuns also wore what looked like six-foot-long rosaries belted around their waists with crucifixes hanging in front.

After hearing from my previous five teachers, my sixth-grade teacher, Sister Mary Elvadine, was mentally prepared to subdue me. I, on the other hand, was fully prepared to be my usual self. The battle lines were drawn! When kids with learning challenges such as these are targeted rather than assisted, they will digress to the lowest opinion and standard expected from them. Our behaviors will, after all, mirror our personal view of ourselves.

One day, as my classmates left the classroom for recess, I took my assigned position in the front of the row. We marched down the hallway, through the doors, and began our descent of two flights of concrete stairs to the ground floor. As we descended, I looked down and noticed the black gown cascading about two or three steps behind my teacher. I wondered for a brief moment what would happen if I stepped on it—and that's all it took. Before I knew it, Sister Elvadine was rolling head over heels down the steps. I stood in amazement as the white hood quickly flashed by several times as Sister Elvadine rolled down those stairs. To my young and frightened mind, the sister reminded me of a giant bowling ball. When she came to rest, I was the first on the scene. I raised the black veil up to see if she was alive. Behind me, I heard the thundering voice of Monsignor O'Sullivan screaming at me. He actually shook his fist at me. From under this mass of black cloth came a muffled voice: "It wasn't him; I tripped on my rosary beads."

> When kids with learning challenges such as these are targeted rather than assisted, they will digress to the lowest opinion and standard expected from them.

The office secretary called an ambulance and Monsignor sent us all outside. The good sister was in the hospital for about two weeks. I was really shaken up, because I hadn't intended to cause her any physical harm—or any harm at all. I just impulsively stepped on her gown. I wonder how often, because of our personal image of ourselves, we impulsively act out against our Lord without taking the time to think of the consequences.

When the sister came back from the hospital, we all watched from the classroom window as she got out of an ambulance. She had a cast on one leg and a body cast with a brace that held her arm parallel to the ground. I felt terrible! I only lived one block from the school, so that evening, I went to the convent to try and visit her.

I knocked on the back door. I believe the nuns were expecting a delivery, so they simply opened the door without asking who was present. I was shocked to see all the nuns in somewhat regular clothes. The hair on their heads was cut very short; in fact, I think one or two of them even shaved their heads. This was a first for me! When they saw me, they were equally panicked, and someone yelled, "It's a child!" as they slammed the door. Then one of the nuns, fully dressed in her habit, came to the door and asked what I wanted. I told her that I wanted to visit Sister Elvadine. The nun left the doorway. After a few moments, she came back and told me to go around to the front of the convent. The sister would see me in the music room. I did as I was told.

As Sister Elvadine came slowly hobbling in, she asked me what I wanted. I remember saying to her "Sister, you lied."

Making no excuses for herself, she simply stated to me, "Joel, as you can see, I cannot carry books to the classroom. I cannot grade papers, nor will I be able to clean erasers and blackboards. Do you know anyone who would be able or willing to help me until I get better?"

Realizing this was my cue, I said, "Of course, I would be more than happy to do that."

The result of the following weeks of service was totally unexpected. When we allow Him to, God does unexpected and great things in our lives. This nun and I not only developed a friendship, but my reputation around the school and the church also changed drastically. It really would not have mattered if I had not finished my grade school years at St. Vincent DePaul. The lesson I learned about having grace and forgiveness for someone else and experiencing a true friendship developed through all of it was worth any sacrifice.

I began to learn what a lifestyle of abiding could be, but it would be many years (and many more impulsive acts of rebellion and defiance) before I would submit to the will of our Father God. If the benefits and union I felt with this nun were so rewarding, how much more would an abiding union with our Redeemer be? The problem faced by most of us is the same as this situation that I faced in sixth grade. We feel, because of our past reputation or lifestyle, that we would never be acceptable to our Lord—but as Doni points out in the rest of this chapter, this could not be further from the real truth.

In meditating on a lifestyle of abiding or remaining in Christ, I thought of the woman in Mathew's gospel who stated to Jesus, "Yes but even the dogs under the master's table, eat the fallen crumbs" (Matthew 15:27). We may not deserve crumbs, but because of what Jesus did for us, we are seated at the table instead of under it. We definitely do not deserve this honor, but as is it is stated in 1 John 3:1, "See what love the Father has lavished on us in letting us be called God's children! For that is what we are." Imagine—we get to sit and eat with the Creator of the universe, because *we are* His children! Is this just going to magically happen, or do we have to do something to deserve it? How do we live our lives as children of God?

Romans 1:17 tells us, "For in it is revealed how God makes people righteous in his sight; and from beginning to end it is through trust." (*Trust* is rendered *faith* in some translations.) The verse goes on to say, "But the person who is righteous will live his life by trust."

Our Father brings us to the place that we cannot reach ourselves—a place of righteousness through trusting in the unbelievable sacrifice Jesus offered for us at the cross. Romans 1:17 says that God makes people righteous. We can't do this! We will never learn to abide in Him without recognizing that we need Him desperately!

What the world teaches us is a wisdom that will always pull us away from the one we desperately need. The world's standards of living, which encourage us to depend on ourselves, are what we are left with. That's not trust, and without trusting that God has our backs, abiding in Him will be impossible. How do I abide or remain in someone I don't know or trust?

In His Word, our Lord promises that He has good things for us. He won't abandon us. Jeremiah 29:11 says, "For I know what plans I have in mind for you, says the Lord, plans for wellbeing, not for bad things; so that you can have hope and a future." This is the God who calls us to come, stay a while, and find rest. Our Lord knows that we are afraid of what we can't see, yet He calls to our hearts. He speaks words of tender love and tells us that we are the ones He desires to spend time with! The standard of this dark world pulls us far from the belief that we have a Father who wants to hold and love us even when we aren't lovable. He desires to calm our hearts and quiet our fears.

You may have heard the story in Scripture of two sisters, Mary and Martha. If you are a Martha, like my precious wife, you would probably agree that with a houseful of guests to feed and care for, there is much preparation to be done. Mary was not one to worry about the logistical issues, such as meal preparation, making sure that everyone had a place to sit at the table, or getting drinks—the usual chores that come with hospitality. Mary chose to sit at the feet of Jesus and soak in every word that He spoke. Martha loved our Lord deeply but was restless and worried that the work would not be done. Frustrated by her sister's lack of assistance, she insisted that Jesus force Mary to help her. In Luke 10:38–42, Jesus did not teach us to neglect our everyday responsibilities with His rather surprising answer but addressed the restless, fearful heart of Martha. He told her there was only one thing that was *essential* and that Mary had chosen it. I don't imagine this sat well with Martha, given the work that still had to be done, but her heart was in desperate need of the peace that comes with abiding in Christ—resting, remaining, and allowing Him to love and soothe her. Jesus knew this.

Our precious Father desires to bring good things to each of us. He pursues us. He longs to spend time with us.

You may, at times, have felt that Jesus is here just to keep us in line, but in truth, what kind of relationship would that cultivate? The one who came to call us His own through the suffering of a horrible death has greater plans for you and me. If we believe that He is here to remind us of all we have done wrong, we are not likely to spend any time abiding in him. I can't imagine a more uncomfortable, unloving relationship than that of constant admonishment and accusations. Such a relationship will not lead to the healing grace that Christ longs to bring. The grace of our Lord understands my restless heart, and He longs to comfort me.

It's true that the nature of man is to find the cookie jar and snatch the cookie, but grace understands this, too. Jesus desires to show us our own hearts. You may ask, "Why would I want Him to do that?" If we trust Him and believe that we are who He wants most, then we can open our hearts to Him and allow Him in. "What if I cannot? How will I ever abide in Him?" This is a huge stumbling block.

Like most folks, I tend to think that I already know what the Father is going to say to me if I show Him my heart. After all, He knows how sinful I can be! Here is the question: <u>is the God of the universe chasing after us just to put us in the corner for a time-out? Really?</u> Who tells us this? The highest price that could ever be paid for you and me was paid at the cross. God wants us to **be** open with our hearts. He wants us to expose them to His truth and light. He wants us to receive all that He has for us—all the forgiveness that the Son could offer us at His cross. God's forgiveness didn't come with a set of rules, and if that is what you are hearing, then you are being lied to! The gift of this relationship does not cost you or me anything; it's free! We *are* the bride of Christ. He is our husband! (Matthew 25:1, 5, 6, 10; Mark 2:19–20; Luke:5:34–35; John 2:9, 3:29)

Abiding in Christ is a two-way street—it's not all us trying to be good and follow the rules. Our Father longs for our friendship. He wants to be a lover—a husband. God's Word says that while I was still sinning, Jesus died for me (Romans 5:8). He meets us more than half way!

Chapter Meditations

1. Are you a Mary or a Martha?

2. Is there something wrong with being a Mary or a Martha?

3. What do you think you would have to do or change in order to have your heart open and to have a vulnerable relationship with your Savior?

4. What blocks you from allowing God into your heart?

CHAPTER FOUR

A Lesson from Ants

Abiding in our actions can be difficult with our hectic schedules and way too many demands. Psalm 141:8 says, "For my eyes are toward You, O God, the Lord: in You I take refuge: do not leave me defenseless."

We will not be left defenseless as long as we keep our eyes focused on our Lord. As Sarah Young states in her book, *Jesus Calling,* "Keeping your eyes on Me (Jesus) is the same thing as trusting Me. It is a free choice that you must make thousands of times daily." These are difficult days, and this is not often easy. We are pulled in many directions, and each tug takes our focus off our ultimate goal—abiding in Him.

A number of years ago, I had an occasion to observe a large red ant colony in a jungle in Southeast Asia. I think we can all learn a valuable lesson from these ants. I can vividly remember every event of this day.

The date was May of 1965. The location was a jungle area in South Vietnam. I was a paratrooper with the 173rd Airborne Brigade (Separate). At this time, I held the rank of Specialist Fourth Class in the United States Army. We were the first army unit to enter Vietnam. Most of us were not seasoned—that is, we had never actually been in a battle. We were on a clearing operation known as a search and destroy mission.

The jungle was hot! The temperature was about 110 degrees; the canopy of trees over us was so thick that we couldn't see the sun. It was almost as though it was dusk or evening, yet the time was actually around noon. The foliage on the jungle floor was thick, and with that canopy above, the jungle actually created its own atmosphere. The air was humid. It was hard to breathe, and the air mixed with many odors from mold to a sweet smell I had never smelled before. The ground was so moist that it allowed nothing to soak in; the afternoon monsoon rains ran off to the nearest river or rice paddy, leaving a muddy slime that was covered by moss and the dense underbrush. This underbrush rose six to ten feet from the earth, and visibility was a maximum of eight feet in front of me. Occasionally, when I could see the tops of the brush, there was a sort of clearing between them and the tops of the trees, which were about eighty feet above us all. That area was filled with twisted vines and a haze or light fog.

Something seemed really eerie! I realized that the normal noises of birds or an occasional monkey had ceased. This was a clue that I would learn to be mindful of in the future. This silence was suddenly broken by a noise I had never before heard, but one I shall never forget. It was as though all hell opened its mouth and roared! I feel someone grab me. It was a sergeant who fought in the Korean War. He pulled me by the arm and yelled, "Get down; we're under fire!" It is only now I realize the noise that held me spellbound for a few seconds was the sound of bullets passing by me, cracking like large firecrackers as they broke the sound barrier.

I saw some soldiers scattered on the ground, lying motionless, their blood mingling with a wet slime on the jungle floor. I crawled to a nearby tree. That same Sergeant crawled on his stomach toward me. Others began yelling, "Return fire! Just open up on them and shoot low." I switched my M16 to fully automatic and began spraying bullets into the brush at an unseen enemy. I emptied two magazines of twenty rounds each. I was reaching for a third magazine to put in my weapon, and I remembered the hand grenades that were strapped to my ammo patches. I took one of the grenades off my pouch and pulled the pin. I let go of the handle and counted about three seconds before throwing it into the brush in front of me. Instinctively, I put my head down and waited for the explosion. I found a moment of peace, like a child who is afraid of the dark and pulls his covers over his head.

I looked up again, and in the midst of all the chaos, I noticed a line of ants—large red ants about half an inch long. There were two columns of them—one marching methodically up my tree and into a one-inch hole in the trunk and another marching out of its sanctuary down the tree and out into the jungle. I became furious with them! I screamed at them as loud as I could, "What is wrong with you? Don't you know there is a war going on?" They seemed to be clueless. They just remained focused on their own world—their own individual and collective tasks.

Aren't we like those ants? We take fire and don't even know it! Tomorrow morning, when your alarm clock goes off, have you figured out how many times you can hit the snooze bar and still make it to work on time? Is your life so completely ordered that you know exactly how much time you can take for breakfast, rush-hour traffic, and maybe a quick cup of coffee on the way to work? As you travel to work, do you recognize the same faces and exchange the same pleasantries? Can you almost anticipate the conversations in the break room? About two hours before quitting time, does your mind begin to plot out how the journey home must be? You plan the stop at the grocery store, the kids' soccer practice, what you're going to fix for dinner, your favorite TV show, and a quick shower. Then you're off to bed in preparation to start all over again tomorrow.

For most of us, that is the way our lives have become. We are in danger of forgetting that there is a war going on all around us. Just like the ants, we become so focused on our own lives—both individually and as a community—that we become complacent and forget that we have a purpose here. This daily march out into the jungle, working out a living, and then returning back to our sanctuary somehow becomes a way of life. We are just like the ants, and it all seems normal!

Have you ever taken your finger or your foot and disturbed a column of ants? They become almost panicked, don't they? They scurry around until they can catch the scent of where they are supposed to be, and then they hurry to catch up with the column in front of them. Isn't this the same thing that we do on a daily basis once we have fallen into the routine of life? This routine is only interrupted on occasion by holidays or special events, but we quickly find our place again and fall in line with the rest of mankind in a routine that is so commonplace, it is accepted by almost everyone as a norm. Squeezed into this routine is a trip to a building we call church. On Sunday, we sing some hymns, listen to a teaching or sermon, throw a tip at God, and go home. Doesn't that fulfill our duty?

This Sunday trip is followed (of course) in the winter by football and in the summer by some activities we call quality time with our children. Is this really what we're supposed to do? Is this the directive that Jesus left us? My belief is that our Lord wants—even expects—us to be different. *We're supposed to stand out, not fit in!* I have been told by some that my thinking is old-fashioned. Well, God is sort of ancient Himself, and I don't believe His thinking has changed at all. The fact is that I know we all become complacent, especially in these times when we have to struggle so hard just to survive. I believe that sometimes, we need to take a look at where we have been in order to see where we are headed. It is like using a compass and taking a back azimuth, which is a 180 degree turn or about face, to make sure that we are on the right path.

There is nothing new under the sun. In Revelation 2–3, Jesus told John how he felt about the churches. Guess what—the exact same struggles and sins in the seven churches Jesus confronted then exist in our church today! I believe our church today mirrors the very first church that Jesus talked about—the church at Ephesus. In Revelation 2:1–4, Jesus said,

To the angel of the Messianic Community in Ephesus write: here is the message from the one who holds the seven stars in his right hand and walks among the seven golden menorahs: I know what you have been doing, how hard you have worked, how you have persevered, and how you can't stand wicked people; so you tested those who call themselves emissaries but are not-and you found them to be liars. You persevered and you have suffered for my sake without growing weary. But I have this against you: you have lost the love you had at first. Therefore remember where you were before you fell, turn from the Sin, and do what you used to do before. Otherwise, I will come to you and remove your menorah from its place-if you don't turn from your sin.

It sounds to me like church at Ephesus became complacent. Perhaps its people fell into a daily routine that was considered the norm! We are not sure what they did, but it's pretty clear what they did *not* do. Can you remember when you first accepted the Lord Jesus as your Savior? Do you remember the feeling you had? Was there a peace that overcame you? Did you have a desire for more of Him in you? For a while, did it seem like everything just fell into place and that all the problems of life seemed to have answers? Do you know that life on this planet is going to get more difficult? What are you going to do? Will working harder or longer hours make it better?

Unfortunately, working harder and longer has become the norm. Husbands and wives both work while we leave the future of our children in the hands of teachers, coaches, day care workers, and even Sunday school teachers. We tell our children that we are working so that we can give them better lives. The real truth is that we don't want to go back where *we* came from. We want more than our parents offered or could afford. I believe there is a fear of the future, because it is changing so quickly, and we can no longer predict what tomorrow will bring. Jesus has an answer to this.

We are called to abide in Jesus in our actions, not to hide from Him or become insensitive. Survival is one of our more basic instincts, and all too often, it has believers looking for a place to hide. What we really should do is place our eyes on Jesus, draw our swords, and take an *offensive* stand against the adversary and this world of his.

Our Lord said in the Scriptures, "I am the way the truth and the life" (John 14:6). In the gospel of John, He stated, "I Am the Resurrection and the Life! Whoever puts his trust in me will live, even if he dies; and everyone living and trusting in me will never die" (John 11:25–26). He said this to everyone. His sacrifice was for all people.

Abiding action is never easy for us. It was not always easy for our Lord. He gave us examples in the Scriptures and showed us how we are to live. He does not expect us to accomplish our actions on earth by ourselves. His actions on earth were accomplished in the same way that He asks us to accomplish them now (John 14:12). Jesus went to the Father and sought out the Father's divine will in everything He did (John 8:28–29). We do not have a heavenly Father who became desensitized to the needs of others and checked out. His every act was divine. Everyone who abides in Him can do the same thing. Our Lord said, "All these things and more you will do because I am going to the Father. (John 14:12)" The problem is that we may often be uncomfortable.

When our Lord came under the criticism of the Pharisees because His disciples picked grains of wheat and ate them on Shabbat (the Sabbath), His disciples were not the only ones picking the grain. Jesus and His disciples were hungry, and they had little. Poverty was not a stumbling block to them. They accepted it, because they abided in our Lord and witnessed the divine work of the Father on earth. *They had little to distract them.* This could be true for us, but the fact is that the more we have, the harder we will have to work to keep it. The times we are in are like none other! The companies and businesses of the world will not give up their profits. The cost share will be put on the backs of the people. We have a choice to make. We can seek the world and what it has to offer and become slaves to it, or we can seek our Lord first. We can seek His kingdom and what He has for us, and righteousness will be ours. I believe His question to us is this: *"Do you want what is fleeting or what is everlasting?"*

We cannot achieve much of the everlasting on earth. It has been saved for us—prepared for us in a future place of abiding with God (John 14:3). For now, we must keep our eyes on Him. Our hearts must desire Him. Then the things of the earth will seem very empty, because they are.

What our Lord says to us is simple. Look at Him! Look at His life on earth. If He had lived in a palace, He would have had to focus on maintaining it. He would have spent the majority of His days in management, not in the deliverance of the oppressed. He wants us to get rid of the earth! We need to take a holy bath and wash the earthly desires down the drain. This one action would greatly minimize pain and suffering. The anxiety and depression most of us experience come from desiring the wrong things. Seeking the things of the earth leads our actions in the wrong direction. If our desire is to be in union with our Lord, then our thoughts will be on Him, and our actions will be as one with His. We will delight the Father, Almighty God, and receive His blessing.

We can see clearly from the Scriptures that when the Father blesses us, we have knowledge and wisdom, which are supernatural and completely filling. People who are of the earth will not understand it any more than they did when our Lord was physically present among us. The beauty is that we won't care about this, because doing the will of Almighty God is worth more than anything we might gain on earth—even if God's will leads to an execution stake (the cross).

<u>Chapter Meditations</u>

1. Do you seek a place to hide, or are you willing to take time to seek out your neighbor, who might be lost or in need?

2. What do you believe God has called you to do in this life?

3. Do you believe that what you have is sufficient? If not, what more do you need or want? If it is sufficient, why?

4. What do you worry about most?

CHAPTER FIVE

Where Our Thoughts Are, Our Hearts Will Be

Today as in times in the past, the thoughts of man unleash the inner desires. If these desires are for the self or personal gratification, they will lead away from our Lord and bring us to ruin. If our desire is to be one with our Lord—to abide in Him—then those thoughts will direct us toward Him. Throughout the Scriptures, the thoughts of man bring destruction. Eve sinned, because her thoughts were impure. When she allowed the thought questioning her right to eat of the tree of Good and Evil to be planted, she became enslaved to the selfish ambition to become like God and have knowledge of good and evil. When she put the thought into action through selfish desire, she ushered in the downfall of mankind. If not for the Father's love, humankind would have ended there.

Eve entertained the thought placed by the adversary, the ancient serpent. Instead of answering his questions and engaging in a conversation with him, she should have rejected his advances and said, "No! I do not want to even talk with you!" If her eyes had been fixed on the rest of the garden and what God gave her, she would not have focused on the tree in the center of the garden. She would have realized what she had and not desired more. She was fully aware of what God had promised if she and Adam ate from the tree in the center of the garden. Her desire was so strong that she was willing to entertain ungodly thoughts and accept a death sentence for a moment of pleasure. How many times have we done this? Our prideful quest for success and our insatiable thirst for the pleasures of the world and self-gratification often direct our thoughts and lead us away from the promised eternal life with our Lord. Nothing has changed since Adam and Eve were in the garden.

Every action begins with a thought. Does a toddler instinctively put his finger into an electric outlet? Perhaps there is a thought: *I wonder what* … When you observe a toddler pointing his finger toward a socket, what is your thought and subsequent reaction? You see, the toddler is experimenting. Our reaction to the toddler's finger is not necessarily based upon personal experience, is it? We have somehow learned this could be a shocking experience. The same is true for sin!

Our Lord wants us to learn from those who have gone before us, from His Word, and from present teachers so that we can act on this learning. There is no need to experience separation from Him through sin. Our Lord wanted us to be able to choose—that is why He put the tree in the center of the garden. The tree was not put there to tempt us! It was not God who tempted, but the adversary! God wanted man to choose Him. He wanted man to choose a relationship with Him over all else. God wanted Adam and Eve to see that He had always and would always continue to take care of them as a loving Father. If a parent attempted to force a child to want and love him or her, how would that work out? Parents are totally gratified when their children freely come to them and give them a hug.

God wanted to take care of his children in the garden, but He wanted them to choose to love Him. This has never changed! God does not send anyone to eternal punishment. That is each individual's choice. It is no different now than it was in the garden—with one major exception. God provided an escape for the punishment we actually deserve through the sacrifice of His Son on the cross. Our Lord paid for the sins of all mankind. He showed us the way. Yes, man does have the knowledge of good and evil, but now he has the knowledge of *total good*. He has the knowledge of abundant goodness and all-consuming love. This love is so great that hell cannot stand against it. This is a love so evident that once it is accepted, it overcomes death and gives new life.

People have knowledge of the truth—the knowledge of an all-consuming love that would and did die for them. Now the choice is not to eat of the fruit of the tree but to open the eyes of our hearts to the beauty of the fruit—to taste it and see that the Lord is sweet. He died so mankind can eat of the fruit of the tree of life. Because of our Lord's life and death on earth, we have a clear choice now between good and evil. We can think on things that are pure and lovely, or we can allow the adversary to darken our thoughts.

Eve's sin was based on raw human desire. We are without excuses. We are blessed to live in a time when we can hear God's voice. We're in a time when we have the ability to read and understand clearly what temptation is. Eve was the first person to be tempted. That powerful pull toward self-gratification had never been experienced before. We have the knowledge of what temptation is and how to overcome it. Our thoughts can lead us in either direction. The choice is ours to make!

In the New International Version of the Bible, the word *thought* appears 157 times. Over half of those are in reference to negative thoughts or thoughts that lead to punishment. I would like to look at the book of James with regard to thoughts. I like the book of James! It gives great counsel on life.

In James 2:11, James talked about the synagogue ruler. In this teaching, a wealthy man and a poor man both entered the synagogue. The leader of the congregation gave a seat of honor to the rich man and had the poor man sit on the floor at the congregation leader's feet. Ungodly thoughts led the synagogue ruler to give a higher place to a rich man.

> Eve was the first person to be tempted. That powerful pull toward self-gratification had never been experienced before.

James pointed out that by this act of distinction, the ruler became a judge with evil motives. This is true! *If our thoughts are not pure, then our actions and speech are evil.* Again in James 2, the author stated, "You believe God is one: the demons do too, and the thought makes them shudder with fear." Thoughts give way to reality in the mind. No act or word comes from man without being preceded by a thought. If a person's thoughts abide with God, then what he does and says will be pleasing to Him. Yes, the demons tremble at the thought of the Father, but a true believer—one who takes his thoughts captive and redirects them to the Father—will have no fear. Death has no sting!

Every selfish act begins with the selfish thought from a selfish motive. It is impossible for man to please the Father and remain in His will while seeking to satisfy the ungodly desires of the self. By its nature, ungodly self-gratification is of earthly desire and gain. Pleasing the Father can bring inner pleasure, but this is first and foremost spiritual in nature. Try to put words to the spiritual satisfaction of seeing any person turn his or her life over to God by accepting salvation through the sacrifice of our Lord on the cross.

Once you witness the freedom a person expresses when he or she has been set free from the bondage that has weighed him or her down over years of servitude to the enemy, you become aware of the fact that there are no human words to adequately express that spiritual joy. If you contrast this, however, with thoughts of earthly desire, then there is a drastic difference in the type of emotion experienced. For instance, if you dream about winning the lottery, you have little trouble describing what you would do with that money. What we are talking about is *earth* versus *eternity.* Where man's thoughts are, there his actions will be. A person has a thought about a sexual act or sexual encounter; then, like a horse with no bit or bridle, his emotions begin to take over and direct his actions. The entire progression of sin all begins with the thought!

In the Bible, we are directed to take our thoughts captive. This does not mean that we wait for an evil thought and fight against it.

It means that *we direct our thoughts toward things that are lovely, pure, and holy.* We keep our minds and our desires on a relationship with our Lord. *As believers in our Lord Jesus, we should be on the offensive against the enemy.* We have total authority over the adversary and his demonic realm through the powerful name of Jesus. The adversary and his demons should tremble in fear and leave when we walk into a room. This is not because we as mortals are anything at all. It is because those of us who accepted our Lord as Savior and were baptized in water and the Holy Spirit have received within us the very spirit of God. We are his temple.

One of the weapons I use often, which places me in a secure spiritual place with my Lord, is mental imagery. I will ask our Lord to show Himself to me. Invariably, he takes me to one of two places. I either imagine I am on the hillside just outside the Mount of Olives or I see the vision St. John had of the Paschal Lamb. This lamb was slain but lived and was worthy to be handed the scroll and open it. When my mind is focused on these things, the adversary has no way to come near me.

In the book of Genesis, man sins against God, so he hides himself from God. Man always wants to hide his sin. His pride causes him to blame others for his own actions rather than taking the responsibility. Adam and Eve had all they needed, but they wanted more! They lusted for more than God had given them. We need to learn to be content with what God has given us. We need to constantly remember that no matter what we may experience on earth, nothing can compare with the fact we are the temple of the very Spirit of God. The same Spirit who breathed our universal existence into being and raised Jesus from the dead is alive within each of us. Through Godly thoughts, we can nurture the existence of the Holy Spirit within us.

Chapter Meditations

1. What reoccurring thoughts might lead you into sinful desires?

2. Are your eyes focused on what you have been given? List some of the blessings God has given to you.

3. You can refuse to entertain impure thoughts when they are placed there by the adversary and his demonic followers. How do you feel you can best accomplish this?

4. What do you think would happen in your life if you made a habit of daily or even hourly refreshing your mind and thoughts by presenting your entire being to Jesus and picturing yourself in His presence?

5. Where do you think you and Jesus would meet if He took you to a private place?

6. Could you start every day by asking our Lord to help you keep your mind pure and holy? If so, when temptation extends a hand to you, would you be able to tell the enemy, "*No,* in the name of Jesus, I command you to leave me!"

7. Will you turn away from the pleasures of this earth and choose to follow Jesus into eternity?

CHAPTER SIX

Mrs. Jacobs

We abide in our Lord in two ways—by meditating on the written and living Word of God and by realizing the power and importance of our own spoken word. In the gospel of Matthew, Jesus stated, "Moreover I tell you the truth: on the Day of Judgment people will have to give an account for every careless word they have spoken; for by your own words you will be acquitted, and by your own words you will be condemned" (Matthew 12:36).

The apostle James added, "Anyone who thinks he is religiously observant but does not control his tongue is deceiving himself, and his observance counts for nothing. The religious observance that God the Father considers pure and faultless is this: to care for orphans and widows in their distress and to keep oneself from being contaminated by this world" (James 1:26–30). James talked about the taming of the tongue. We must also tame the ears. In these days, you will see and hear about many things that are horrifying and ugly. Pain and suffering will be all around you. Do not speak of them! If your mind and heart are united with the Father, your desire will be to live in purity and holiness. As Doni stated previously, when we allow these things into our minds, they will provide patterns for our thoughts, words, and perhaps even actions.

James continued his discourse on the tongue in James 3:4–12:

> Or take ships as an example. Although they are so
> large and are driven by strong winds, they are steered
> by a very small rudder wherever the pilot wants to go.
> Likewise the tongue is a small part of the body, but it
> makes great boasts. Consider what a great forest is set
> on fire by a small spark. The tongue also is a fire, a
> world of evil among the parts of the body. It corrupts
> the whole person, sets the whole course of his life on
> fire, and is itself set on fire by hell. All kinds of animals,
> birds, reptiles and creatures of the sea are being tamed
> and have been tamed by man, but no man can tame the
> tongue. It is a restless evil, full of deadly poison. With
> the tongue we praise our Lord and Father, and with it
> we curse men, who have been made in God's likeness.
> Out of the same mouth comes praise and cursing. My
> brothers, this should not be. Can both fresh water and
> salt water flow from the same spring? My brothers, can
> a fig tree bear olives, or a grapevine bear figs? Neither
> can a salt spring produce fresh water.

My wife, Doni, and I have counseled and ministered in the areas
of spiritual warfare and inner healing for many years. Some of the
most wounded people are not the ones who have necessarily done
sinful things but those who were cut down and destroyed by parents
and loved ones. People who were supposed to speak life actually spoke
curses and death. The real problem is that these very people, who were
given the responsibility to demonstrate the love of God to their precious
children by allowing the flow of living water to wash over them, instead
drowned their children with words of guilt, shame, unforgiveness, and
condemnation.

These wounded people struggle through life, wondering what a
good God looks like. They ask themselves why others succeed and

they continually fail, not realizing that the thoughts and memories of the past continue to dictate the behaviors of the present, thus directing the outcome of the future. This is not the life that God intended for any of His children to live. We must remember that we have an omnipresent God who is everywhere and with everyone at the same time. He was present with

> Some of the most wounded people are not the ones who have necessarily done sinful things but those who were cut down and destroyed by parents and loved ones.

us when we were scourged by an evil tongue, and He grieved with us. He was also present with us for laughter and rejoiced with us over our successes.

In almost all of the cases where parents were the destroyers, they actually did the very best job they could, even though they were destructive. There is no how-too book that accompanies each child's birth. Parents are left to rely upon what they were taught or shown in their own wounded pasts. Thus, on a secular level, you can plainly observe the working of what is referred to in the spiritual realm as generational curses. Once in a while, we have encountered situations where parents did know better but selfishly hated the fact that they had children and allowed their venomous words and actions to kill the joy within their children. Although this has become more prevalent in recent years, the situation is present in the minority of cases.

I believe that most parents, given the blessing of age and wisdom, will in some way seek forgiveness and attempt to heal the relationship with their children. This is all well and good if the child has not passed on the regrettable behavior to yet another generation. There is work for those of us who have lived enough of life to admit our errors and realize, through the grace of God, that we must find a way to correct them.

In my early years, I was a typical American male. I was a young lion and thought I had it all together when in fact, I had nothing. Well, that is not entirely true. I did have a very large dose of pride bordering on arrogance, which always works to aid in destructive behaviors. I made one of the most common mistakes any young American male can make. I hardly ever sought the counsel of wiser, older men and never accepted counsel without seeking it first. Like most, I looked for help when I was in a corner and had no way out. I was taught that once out on my own, I had to make my own decisions and stand by them. Well, this is true, but those decisions would be healthier if additional input—perhaps from someone who already walked the same path—were taken into the equation first.

Destructive words, coupled with a lack of understanding and support, shot fiery darts straight from the quiver of the adversary, wounded my heart, and destroyed the image of God within me. I was unable to see myself as God saw me, and for many years, the course He had for me was changed. If we allow God's work to redirect our way, He will heal the events of the past and give us a new picture of His hand working in them.

Remember the story of my second-grade teacher? She was one of only two lay teachers in the school. Twenty-seven years later, I had an occasion to be at St. Vincent DePaul School. I walked through the hall and heard someone call out my name. I turned, and there was Mrs. Jacobs. With tears in her eyes, she exclaimed, "Thank God, I have been praying I would see you again." She went on to tell me that she was the principal of the school. When she taught my second-grade class, she was right out of college. She was prepared to teach, but no one was prepared for me. She told me that by the end of the year, she realized that I had something going on that was not a behavior problem. That summer, she went to California and spent the entire summer learning about a new problem called ADHD. As a result of her dedicated work to help parents and teachers understand and deal with this disorder, that school became a leader in the field of dealing with ADHD within the private school sector.

Imagine how this made me feel. It was bittersweet—mostly sweet. This is a clear example that what the enemy intended for evil, God used for good. It would not have happened if Mrs. Jacobs did not have her eyes on our Lord or recognize something was wrong. If her thoughts had not sought God's thoughts, she would not have realized that her words did not speak life. Her conscience would not have been seared. She would never have been led to seek the answers that she found in California, and the children who followed after me and became successful would have had to walk a much different path.

You may ask, "Does this make what I had to live through somehow better?" The answer is yes—not just because of the outcome at St. Vincent DePaul, but also because I can see the hand of God over my life from that time. I am very thankful that we were able to make amends. Mrs. Jacob's first words to me—"I have been praying I would see you again"—were very important. She had prayed for someone she knew she had harmed. God always answers our prayers! What about my heart, though? I can tell you that I had not prayed for her. My bad!

As long as we harbor unforgiveness for someone, every time something happens to remind us of that person or event, the memory of the past and the anger, hate, or bitterness associated with it will have control over that portion of our lives. What do—or should—you do when the adversary reminds you of someone from the past whose tongue spewed venomous words at you?

> As long as we harbor unforgiveness for someone, every time something happens to remind us of that person or event, the memory of the past and the anger, hate, or bitterness associated with it will have control over that portion of our lives.

Chapter Meditations

1. Have you been wounded by a friend or loved one who spoke words that hurt you?

2. Were the words spoken to you true (in whole or in part)?

3. Have you forgiven this person? How do you feel the Lord would have you approach him or her to seek forgiveness and restoration?

4. List the persons who have spoken hurtful words to you.

5. Ask the Lord to help you pray a prayer of forgiveness toward each person who hurt you. Ask Him to break the tie to that memory and pass blessings on instead. When the adversary reminds you of these people, remind him that you have forgiven them, and pray for these people again. The enemy of God hates it when we pray for people we are supposed to hate.

6. Are there others to whom *you* have spoken words of destruction?

7. How can you seek their forgiveness?

CHAPTER SEVEN

Thoughts Lead to Behavior

I believe that our thought patterns can be the single most potent weapon in the enemy's arsenal. For this reason, my wife and I always encourage anyone who comes to us for help to begin reading the Bible. We ask people to read at least one chapter every day before they leave their homes. The Bible is a love story, not a set of rules. It demonstrates God's unconditional love for us. The authors of the Scriptures composed testimonies of themselves and others who responded to that love, highlighting how life changes when we abide in God's grace. When we read Scripture and meditate on God's Word, our thought patterns are directed toward Him. Subsequently, our behaviors cause our Lord to look upon us and say, "I love you. Well done, good and faithful servant."

Keeping our thoughts pure and holy can be a lifelong battle. The adversary constantly attempts to bring to my mind memories of the past that could alter my view of myself and thus refocus my behaviors. When this occurs, I acknowledge that those memories are true—I used to live a life of sin, fed by impure sexual desires and motives. However, I then remind the adversary that I have taken these things before the Father, and through the grace of our Lord Jesus and the blood that He shed for me on the cross; I have been forgiven and redeemed. I then refocus my mind and thoughts on the new pattern of life God gave me. This is a huge issue for everyone. The adversary would like to have us all believe that there is no hope—that what we did in the past defines who we are and how we should behave. This could not be further from the truth!

The rest of this chapter is devoted to demonstrating how we can overcome this obstacle of allowing our past to define who we are. My precious wife, Doni, struggled with this issue for many years. The memories of some of the events of her childhood were so powerful that they caused her to form a negative belief about herself and a pattern of life that was certainly not what God intended for her. She came through this and is victorious, and she now shares her thoughts with us in an effort to help us all redirect our thoughts and behaviors toward God.

Romans 6:17 states, "By God's grace, you, who were once slaves to sin, obeyed from your heart the pattern of teaching to which you were exposed; and after you had been set free from sin, you became enslaved to righteousness." The pattern by which the readers of Paul's letter led their lives changed.

Romans 6:13 states, "And do not offer any part of yourselves to sin as an instrument for wickedness. On the contrary, offer yourselves to God as people alive from the dead, and your various parts to God as instruments for righteousness." I asked myself, "Do I see the true pattern of my life? If I laid it under the pattern that God has for me, would it look the same? Would it be a pattern of teaching that the world has given me or a pattern that God gave me?"These questions caused me to examine my actions and my thoughts. Christian lives are often under a microscope. Our thoughts are hidden from plain view, and we fail to realize what ungodly thought patterns do and where they take us. Our thoughts are often born out of the familiar areas of our lives—the patterns that were set a long time ago. Since our thought life can influence us greatly in our walk with Christ, changing ungodly thoughts and taking them captive becomes vital!

Let's view our thoughts as patterns for a moment. Do they speak life? Do they tell us that we are new creations in Christ? If we have a pattern of ungodly thoughts that lead us into dark places and separate us from a loving Father, then we have a problem. I'm talking about *patterns*—the things we do on a consistent basis. Why are these so important? Paul spoke of taking our thoughts captive in 2 Corinthians 10:4–5: "Because the weapons we use to wage war are not worldly. On the contrary, they have God's power for demolishing strongholds. We demolish arguments and every arrogance that raises itself up against the knowledge of God; we take every thought captive and make it obey the Messiah." Paul recognized that our thoughts can be a matter of warfare. That is how important they are!

We may have patterns of thinking that stem back to childhood, with some bringing bitter memories. These thoughts can set us up for failure; they oppose what God says about us in his Word. Surprisingly enough, they become patterns. For example, a woman who was a victim of incest as a young girl may have come to believe she could only be loved if she allowed herself to be used sexually. This pattern of thinking could set her up for a lifestyle of ungodly sexual behaviors as an adult.

In Romans 6:17, Paul talked about a new pattern of teaching to which the Romans were exposed. He reminded them that once they obeyed this teaching *from their hearts,* they were set free. This could not have been easy for them; we read in verse 19 that the Romans made a practice of offering themselves to impurity and lawlessness, which enslaved them. However, once they were willing to be *re-taught,* they were set free from unrighteousness. The important point we must grasp from the change in the Roman believers is their *willingness* to think differently about themselves and learn a new way of living. It may be difficult to see that our thought patterns lead us in ungodly behavior, because they are so familiar to us that they've become the very foundation on which our lives are built.

If you set out to construct a building, the first place to begin (once the ground has been excavated) is with a solid foundation on which the structure will be built. This foundation must be straight and level as well as solid, or there is a chance the building will be compromised and may not function as it was intended. If our thoughts about ourselves become our foundation, are they healthy? Do I function as God intended, or have I compromised myself through my thoughts?

I mentioned earlier that thought patterns that stem from childhood can bring bitter memories and lead us toward destructive behavior—especially if they don't line up with what God's Word says about how He views His children. These early thoughts can be viewed as our foundation. I used this principle to line up my own patterns of thinking regarding how I view myself and how God views me. I have provided an example below of what I said about myself and what God said about me.

What I Said about Myself	What God Says about Me
- Because of my past, I am not worth loving.	But God demonstrates His own love for us in that the Messiah died on our behalf while we were still sinners (Romans 5:8).
	Love is patient and kind, not jealous, not boastful, not proud rude or selfish, not easily angered, and it keeps no record of wrongs (1 Corinthians 13:4–5).
- God is angry with me because of what I've done.	
	- Before I formed you in the womb, I knew you; before you were born, I separated you for myself (Jeremiah 1:5).
- God has forgotten about me.	For you fashioned my inmost being, you knit me together in my mother's womb.
	I thank you because I am awesomely Made, wonderfully, your works are Wonders—I know this very well (Psalm 139:13–14).
- I don't feel important.	
	- I tell you in the same way, there will be more joy in heaven over one sinner
- I'm not important enough for God to care whether I repent or not.	who turns to God from his sins than over ninety-nine righteous people who have no need to repent (Luke 15:7).

Chapter Meditation

Write out the thoughts you repeat about yourself. Then go to the Lord in prayer; fix your eyes on Him. Ask Him if this is the way He thinks of you, and write down what He tells you. I think you will be surprised by His view of you.

CHAPTER EIGHT

Dumpster to Doctor

When I was about eight years old, my brother, Larry, bought a Wham-O slingshot. It was made out of solid wood and was powerful enough to shoot arrows from. I asked my dad if I could have one, and of course, he said no. He cited the dangers of them and said that I was too young to have one. Because I was resourceful, I took a couple of coat hangers, wove them together, and using a two thick rubber bands from my father's office, I created my own slingshot. I then went outside to my pretend jungle, the backyard.

I ran from bush to bush and finally crawled on my stomach to the corner of the garage. I saw a dove land on the ground next to a hedge at the side of our house. I picked up a large rock, put it inside the pouch of the slingshot, and took aim at the bird. Just then, the thought came to my mind that I did not want to kill the bird, so I discarded the large rock and picked up a small stone. I took aim again at my prey, only this time, not wanting to hit the bird, I aimed a little high. If you know anything about trajectory, you know I did exactly the right thing to inflict a death sentence on this bird. My homebuilt slingshot proved to be deadly accurate as the stone found its mark, breaking the bird's neck.

I had watched this bird and its mate all summer. I knew doves mated for life. I felt like a murderer. The second my brother, Larry, got home from work, I showed him the bird and told him what I had done. He shrugged and said something like, "It's only a bird."

Ten years later, after a few combat experiences, I no longer felt anything. I had grown to look forward to killing—but I did not take aim at birds. The innocent kid who cried for an entire afternoon because he had killed a dove had changed, and he knew it! I actually did not want to come back from Vietnam. When I found out that I would be med-evacuated home due to a wound that would not heal, I actually went AWOL from the hospital. I am perhaps the only person to have a Military Police escort out of combat.

The battle in which I received these particular wounds was in an area known as the Iron Triangle. My entire battalion was committed, and we knew we were going in against a well-trained North Vietnamese (NVA) unit. In those days, we did not have the luxury of GPS systems, and we relied on maps and a compass to get us to our desired location. We were to land by helicopter in a rice paddy and then move into the jungle against the NVA unit. We were to attack on three sides, converging on the enemy force.

It became very evident there was an error in judging the landing zone. Instead of being dry, we jumped out of the choppers into a rice paddy, chest-deep in water. We had not only landed in the wrong location, but also come in directly in front of the NVA unit. The North Vietnamese soldiers waited until the second group of choppers came in and then opened fire. The fighting was so intense that we could not get any medevac choppers.

We fought in a horseshoe formation so we could give protection to our wounded. The medics placed the wounded on ponchos so they could float, as the rice paddy reeds gave some support and kept them from drowning. The medics had to continually move the injured as the reeds began to give under their weight.

I took my fire team to the left flank, and we assumed a fire position against the bank of the canal that fed the paddy with water. It was about ten to fifteen feet wide and flowing heavily. The NVA were on the opposite side of the canal. At the far end of the canal was a concrete machine gun bunker. We kept killing the gunner, but the NVA would bring another recruit (who was most likely a farmer who had been solicited into their service). Finally, we called in an air strike. We were sent an A1E Skyraider (a WWII plane). We loved those planes, because they could hit targets with more accuracy than the jets of those days.

As the pilot came around and began his assault on the bunker, he flew straight down the canal. He began by opening fire on the position with his wing guns. I heard a voice say, "Joel, put your head down." I could not believe I had heard anything. The noise during an engagement is so loud that you would not be able to hear the guy lying next to you even if he shouted at the top of his voice.

As a bullet passes by, there is what is known as a bow wave report. It is caused by the speed the bullet is traveling and sounds like a large firecracker going off next to your ear. Imagine the sound of thousands of those combined with your own rifle fire, mortar rounds, and hand grenades. Yet I again heard the same voice. This time, it was not a suggestion; it was a command. "Joel, put your head down now!" Everything inside me wanted to continue firing, but I had to obey this commanding voice.

When I opened my eyes, I was under water. I stood up, and to my amazement, I was clear out in the middle of the rice paddy. I instinctively began heading back to my position. I knew I had been wounded again. I was bleeding from both ears. I had received a bullet wound to my arm earlier, and a piece of shrapnel had pierced through my right sinus and lodged under my eyeball. I remember passing a guy lying on a poncho who was beginning to sink. I pulled him over to a fresh area and kept moving back to my position. When I got there, there was nothing but carnage. Apparently as the A1E opened with its wing guns, a bomb that was not loaded properly came loose from the chute and dropped directly in front of us. It nearly took out my entire platoon. I located my steel pot (the helmet of the day), and it was inverted. The barrel of my M16 was bent and curved to the left. There is no doubt in my mind that if I had not obeyed that voice, whatever hit my helmet would have cut my head in half.

You would think after an ordeal like this, I would realize I had heard the voice of God—or at the least, one of His angels—and become a priest or pope. When you are filled with hate, the love of God does not seem tangible.

I returned to the United States, and I was set on a path of self-destruction. I spent a total of three months in the hospital. Upon being discharged, I began drinking heavily. I took my honorable discharge from the military in 1967 and became a police officer for the City of Littleton, Colorado. I met a young lady who was one of the few people willing to listen to me and allow me to unload some of the horror I had locked inside. Most people in those days would not listen to a veteran, but I really needed someone I could talk to who would not judge me. I had found that with this woman, and in my declining mental state, I confused this need with love. We married, but in my heart, I knew that something was really wrong.

> When you are filled with hate, the love of God does not seem tangible.

In 1968, I joined the Denver Police Department; shortly thereafter, my marriage ended. I was totally out of control. I was drinking heavily again and dating a lot of different women. I became involved with another police officer's wife. This resulted in my voluntarily leaving the department, because this officer worked in the same district and was assigned to the same detail as I was. I asked our Division Chief to transfer me, and he refused to do it, telling me to return to duty the next day or resign. I wrote out my resignation that evening.

Through a series of events, I ended up living in a one-room apartment in the same area that I had been working. I didn't feel that I could be any lower—not because of where I was living but because of what I had become. One night, I finally decided to take my own life. I got my .357 Magnum, put the barrel in my mouth, cocked the hammer, and began to squeeze the trigger. I was seated on my couch, and I took a last look around the room. All I had were a few work clothes, a clock radio, and three books.

As I looked around the room for what I believed would be the last time, the thought came to my mind that I had not read one of the three books. I set the gun down on the coffee table with the hammer still cocked. I walked across the room, picked up the book, and said to myself, "Where would I even begin to read this?" The book was the Bible. I simply flipped the cover open and began reading about a guy by the name of David (1 Samuel and 2 Samuel). I quickly learned that this man had committed every sin I had ever committed. Yet because he sought God's forgiveness and earnestly attempted to follow God's will, he was not only forgiven, but also known as a man after God's own heart. This is where I had always wanted to be, but having been raised in a very legalistic denominational church, I did not know it was attainable. I felt an inner peace as I realized that if this man could make it, there was hope for me as well. I now know there is hope for anyone! I made up my mind that I was going to read the entire book cover to cover.

I sat down and began reading through the book of Genesis. As I did, I began to see the immense love God has for us and how He created us so He could enjoy our unity with Him. I was brought back to a sense of reality by a rather loud noise outside my window. I realized that the sun was up, and my balcony was filled with birds waiting for me to feed them. I looked over my shoulder, and the .357 was still cocked on my coffee table. I had read all night, and it had seemed like only moments. For the first time in my life, I knew who Jesus really is—Yeshua, my salvation and Messiah.

I earnestly attempted to change my way of living. I spent three to four hours a night reading the Scriptures and praying. I realized some very important truths. First of all, my sins were not just against others, but also against God. Second, God forgave everything I had done through the atoning, sacrificial death of His own Son on a cross for me. I found overwhelming joy, even though I had nothing.

I could only afford one meal about every three days. I discovered (as did most of us who lived in poverty on East Colfax) that the dumpster at McDonald's had an entire menu to choose from. Unfortunately, although most of this food had not even been touched and was still in wrappers, the health department did not see it this way and forced McDonald's to put locks on their dumpsters. This placed unbelievable hardship on me, and others. I can remember walking around the parking lot of the White Spot Restaurant on East Colfax and Pearl St, looking for a dime. I would then go inside and order a cup of coffee (yes, it was just ten cents then). I would drink the coffee and then fill the cup with cream and as much sugar as I could stomach and drink it. I knew this would probably be all I would have to sustain me for perhaps that entire day. Still, because of the trials I lived through, I learned to really place my trust in Jesus and follow Him. I found inner peace that really did surpass all human understanding. I have gone from those dumpsters to being a Doctor—but not by my own strength. I could never have done it on my own! It has all been through Jesus, who strengthens me.

Because I read the Bible every day, I developed an inner drive to live my life according to the teachings found in the Scriptures. I knew I had to try and find all those I had harmed and seek their forgiveness. One of the blessings I am very thankful for is that the police officer whose wife I had become entangled with accepted my repentance and forgave me. Only by developing a personal relationship with our Lord Jesus and realizing the depth of His love and mercy can we muster the strength to face our accusers and admit that we willfully wronged them. Selfish ambition will only lead to sin and disgrace, but to even attempt to live a selfless life, as our Master modeled for us, can only lead us into the loving arms of a forgiving God.

For many who were raised as Christians, the concept of such a loving God is as foreign as it was to me. I believe that for many, the root of this is that we never witnessed undeserved and unconditional love as children. I believe sight is one of the strongest senses that help children learn. If children do not witness parental love, it is very difficult for them to grasp the idea of a God who could love them so much that He would sacrifice His own Son in order to have a relationship with them.

This world is not easy. It is filled with trials, and as the tribulation described in Matthew chapter 24 nears, these trials will intensify. The situations that we all face—such as death, disease, natural disasters, or loss of homes or jobs—are not acceptable to God. They are not part of the nature of God. Our God is a God of order, not chaos. This is why there is so much unrest in our spirit over these matters, because they are not acceptable to the nature of the God within us. We seek answers to these tragedies and hardships of life. When we cannot find these answers, all too often, our choice is to curse God Almighty or turn away from Him and buy into the lie that a good God would not allow this to happen. The truth is that our good God did not allow suffering to happen before sin entered the world. That same good God still grieves with us and desires something more for us. He can only move in a positive way in our lives when we unite ourselves with Him, and we can only accomplish this by accepting the gift of Jesus' sacrifice on the cross.

In the times we are entering, the only real answers will be found by those whose eyes are fixed on Jesus and whose hearts are united with God Almighty. When we accept our circumstances and expect God to help us with them, then the Father can move in our lives. He will help either with understanding, acceptance, or change. Once a person unites with the Triune God, regardless of circumstances or position in life, he remains in the presence of the Father God Almighty. We stand in the Holy of Holies when we unite our will with God's will.

> This world is not easy. It is filled with trials, and as the tribulation described in Matthew chapter 24 nears, these trials will intensify.

Our circumstances are part of *this* world. If our eyes are focused upon the next world, we will not feel *driven* to fix the issues of this one. Instead, we allow our Lord to fix us. Our focus is then internal, not external. It is eternal, not temporary. When we abide in our Lord Jesus and do not seek our own self-gratification, we can be used by Him to show the abiding love the Father has for everyone. If you want to be shown how this can be true, the best example we have is the Son of God himself.

It was not easy for our Lord to accept the cup prepared for Him. His human nature wanted nothing to do with it. He knew what was imminent. He asked the Father to let the cup pass from Him—but only if it was the Father's will. It was not! By that time in Jesus' human existence, He was one with the Father. He sought the Father's will in all things and thus united with Him. Even in the many trials He had in His ministry, He had to seek the Father first. Then, as now, He could not teach or reach the hearts of people as long as they held on to their personal beliefs and agendas.

Look at the number of times Jesus' disciples turned away or heard His words but did not absorb what He said. They viewed and heard everything through their own filters. They twisted what our Lord did and said to fit their own desire. Once He completed His work by uniting completely with the Father through His glorious resurrection, they understood. Then they were also willing to stand in the presence of the Father and accept the hard times they faced. Because they did this, fruit was born (1 Corinthians 4:9–13).

The many trials of the early church and the hardships its members faced are recorded as examples for us to follow. Early Christians left their mothers, fathers, brothers, sisters, and homes to follow our Lord into the kingdom. Once they took their eyes off the world, they were able to minister with the Almighty God, because they put off everything this world had to offer and took on the mantle of salvation. The Father will take care of everyone and make our paths straight once we unite ourselves with Him. This is not a prosperity promise.

A path becomes straight when we can see the end of the journey. It is not necessarily without curves, potholes, or maybe some detours. Once on that path, we really know what it means to love our neighbors, because we can fully love ourselves. We will love who and what we are, because we will become friends with the Holy Spirit. We will come to a point of trusting the Spirit and the Father and accepting Jesus' love and sacrifice for us. Now we can share our love with our neighbors, because our love is the same as God's love for them.

Unity with God is the gift offered at the cross of our Lord Jesus. He will offer it to all, but He will not force anyone to accept it.

To truly abide in real, pure love, we must first learn to live in the presence of the Almighty Father God. Then we must reach out from the Holy Spirit within us to those around us who are in need. We must seek and save the lost, as we have been instructed to do.

We are told that we are supposed to preach the good news of our Lord to a dying world. While this is very true, I would like to interject a word of caution. Heidi Baker, the selfless missionary to Africa, made a statement in an interview that impacted me greatly. She stated, "Yes, we are to preach the good news. Well, the good news to a starving child is that there is food available. The good news to a homeless man or woman is that there is shelter. The good news to someone who is sick or dying is that there is healing or hope available."

At the end of the day, can we feel that person's pain? Can we look into his or her eyes and see the spirit? Can we pray a prayer for that person that would shake the heavens? All these things and more are possible—that was the promise of our Lord. There are two criteria we need to meet.

> A path becomes straight when we can see the end of the journey.

First, we must be void of self-entanglements. If we have any ungodly self-desire, self-gratification, or pride, then we cannot stand in the presence of the Father and allow His blessing and purpose to flow through us to that other person. Second, we must seek the Father's will for that person. Once we see what that will is, then can we pray in agreement with the Father.

Is it easy to give up the things of this world? Is it easy to deny the flesh and do without? The obvious answer is no. In our human nature, it is not natural to deny the pleasures we naturally seek. We must remember that our nature is linked to fallen man; therefore, we naturally tend to gratify that sinful side of ourselves. But we have another nature—another side—that was created in God's likeness and image. This nature was unlocked for us as Jesus dropped the last drop of blood from His precious body on the cross. The Holy of Holies was opened to us, and God Almighty invites us to come in and abide with Him. The choice is ours.

Chapter Meditations

1. How did you view yourself before reading this chapter?

2. How do you view yourself now?

3. What things stand between you and the Father?

4. List the things you have that you will take into the next world.

5. Write out what you believe the people who know you would say about you, if he or she was writing your epitaph.

6. What do you think that Jesus would say about you?

7. If you lay all worldly stuff down and actively choose to follow Jesus, how will your life be different?

8. Do you think you serve the Lord in your present occupation? Could you bring His light into your work environment?

CHAPTER NINE

Bravo Company: Bloody, but Not Beaten

"The things that come out of the mouth come from the heart. For out of the heart come evil thoughts, murder, adultery, sexual immorality, theft, false testimony, slander" (Matthew 15:18–19). Jesus warned us about this, because we have inherited a sinful nature—a nature that is always self-seeking and self-gratifying. I believe it is impossible to have true, unconditional love for ourselves or for another without first accepting Jesus as Savior and then asking for and receiving the Holy Spirit, who is our counselor.

In the gospel of John, Jesus said that He is the vine and we are the branches. If we remain *in* Him, we will bear much fruit. He states that apart from Him, we can do nothing! Just how are we a part of Him? Accepting Him and His wonderful sacrifice on the cross opens the gate of heaven to us, but what unites us with Him?

In the book of Acts, Jesus told the apostles that He must leave but would send His Spirit, the Counselor, to remain with us—and indeed He did. He entered and empowered all who were in the upper room at the time, and that same power was then given freely to all who came to believe. It is given freely to us today. Abiding love is our Lord's unconditional love for us, and it flows freely from the Holy Spirit. The key word is *unconditional*. Man can love, because he was created in the image of the Almighty God, but his inherited nature as a son of Adam will always get in the way. That nature is the pull that draws us to be self-seeking and self-gratifying.

> You do not have to love a person to forgive him or her; you need to love our Lord!

It is curious how hard we fight for success and how we quickly accept the accolades for it, but just as quickly blame failure on someone or something else. Our lives are like smoke; they are here and then gone—blown by the winds of time, never to be remembered. There is much talk today of carbon footprints. This present age will vanish, but our spiritual footprint will last into eternity. No one—not one person—will escape the judgment of the Father. That judgment is final, and it is eternal. He cannot take back His Word. He can and will only proclaim the truth about the lives we have lived.

For our Lord, truth and forgiveness are linked together. You do not have to love a person to forgive him or her; you need to love our Lord! You need to love Him more than yourself—more than any offense committed against you. Remember, unforgiveness holds you captive and subject to hate. It also holds you captive to the person who harmed you. Every time an event or memory of that person comes to your mind, your heart is filled with anger, and you will relive that past event. We cannot bow down and worship our Lord when our hearts are filled with anger and hatred.

Through forgiveness, we are set free from the chains that bind us to the past. There are people who actually want to hold on to the memories of these events. Some have told me they feel it will protect them from ever having the same experience happen again. Others simply do not want to forgive. They desire to hold on to this pain. The truth is that if our eyes are on Jesus and our direction in this life is toward eternal life with Him, these painful events will most likely not happen again. Holding on to the past is a strategy of the adversary that will keep us nailed to a cross we do not have to carry.

I learned this by spending years consumed with hate and anger. During this time, my family learned how to survive, not live. In those early years, my children never witnessed the love I had for them—the love I now try to show to them. I was filled with hate. My life was directed by the memories of the past, and all they really knew was how angry I could become. All this was rooted primarily in my combat experiences. Soldiers do not return to their loved ones as they left them. They leave parts of themselves on the battlefield and carry memories of what was and dreams of what might have been with them.

In 1965, I was a member of the 173rd Airborne Brigade (Separate), 503rd Infantry. We were the first major Army unit to enter Vietnam. My company was named Bravo Bulls. In the first year of combat, we were given the nickname Bloody Bravo. An *Albuquerque Tribune* article about my company dated April 18, 1966, titled "Meet Bravo Company: Bloody But Not Beaten" said,

> They call it Bloody Bravo here, and the name fits like a grape skin. Last May a Bravo Sergeant became the first casualty for the 173rd Airborne Brigade. Since then the beleaguered men from B Company have spilled enough blood in the jungles of Viet Nam to beggar the imagination.

> They have more Purple Hearts than salt tablets ... some 110 have gotten one, dozens have two a few three, and one, Jacob Rosado of New York, has four—one each for arm, leg, shoulder and chest wounds. Such is the mortality rate, in fact,

Soldiers do not return to their loved ones as they left them. They leave parts of themselves on the battlefield and carry memories of what was and dreams of what might have been with them.

that of 180 men on the original company roster, only 66 are left and of them only 26 have survived unmarked. All six of the original officers have departed—either on carry-all's or otherwise. Nine sergeants have been killed or evacuated. One platoon has gone through three lieutenants. The Company is now under its fifth captain. The First Platoon alone has been down to 10 survivors or less three times. In January they lost 28 in one single two hour battle."

I was not one of the twenty-six who survived unharmed. The truth is that no soldier survives combat unharmed.

As I mentioned previously, I was medically evacuated from Vietnam due to combat wounds. The second hospital I was transported to outside Vietnam was located in San Francisco. I have two very vivid memories of my stay there. After dreaming of a big, cold glass of whole milk, I drank my first glass in several months and promptly became very ill. I am pretty sure it was the milk, but it may have been the bear claw I woofed down along with it.

The second event was much more significant, because it was the first flashback I experienced. A garbage truck picked up a dumpster just outside the hospital. I casually glanced at the driver and then had to quickly look again, because at first glance, he appeared to be Vietnamese. I immediately experienced the same mental responses I had in Vietnam. I found myself in a fight-or-flight mentality. This was just a sampling of what life was to be.

For many years, I drove along roads and did not even realize that I was mentally driving in a jungle setting, looking for the enemy in trees. I sometimes drove for a few miles and did not remember the real road I had driven. I only slept for three or four hours each night. At night, I woke dripping in sweat, although I rarely remembered what I dreamt. My anger and rage were uncontrolled. I could—and often would—erupt in a violent state when provoked.

The remarkable thing about all this is that I thought it was normal. I could describe many other behaviors and events, but I think the picture has been painted. I returned from serving my country and carried both physical and mental scars. I underwent years of counseling and retraining from the Veterans Administration, which helped me to learn to *control* all this, but these things did not heal it. *The healing for any of life's hurts must come from the ultimate healer, our Lord.* Finally, one day, I asked Jesus to help me. Man had done all that was possible.

I had always labored under the assumption that my issues were the memories of the actual battles. What Jesus showed me was that the root to all this was unforgiveness. Jesus asked me one simple question: "If a foreign country came into the United States, what would you do?" The answer was obvious; I would fight to defend it. This is exactly what the Viet Cong did. Their political ideology did not play a role here. It was the purpose given for our involvement in their country's affairs, but the fact remains that we invaded their country. Through this realization and the prayers that followed, I began a process of forgiveness, which in turn led to a release from the chains that had bound me for so many years. The demon of hate and anger no longer had a legal right to me and had to leave. What then remained was a need to repent and ask my loved ones to forgive me for the many times I showed them anger instead of mercy and hatred instead of love.

During those years, although I was able to complete a master's degree and attempt to minister to many people, my family had to wonder why I could not treat them as I did strangers who came to me for help. The answer to this is simple—I did not abide with the Lord. I knew Him, professed Him, and preached a good lesson about Him, but He could not abide where I was. My heart was too full of anger and death to allow Him to enter. I thank the Lord Jesus for His patience and mercy. I thank Him for giving me the time and opportunity to open my heart to Him alone so He can now abide in me and His love can now flow to those around me.

As I wrote this, I experienced many emotions—mostly sorrow. I have also shed tears as I remembered the soldiers who died while under my direction as a nineteen-year-old sergeant. It is a grievous human error to think that we have not been healed or something else remains because we once again *feel* emotions such as these. No, the fact is that we are human, and we will grieve loss. Our Lord shed many tears. To weep as we remember people we lost—people we harmed or who harmed us—is not a sign of weakness. It is not a signal to put up a wall of stone around that part of our heart. It is a sign we *really* understand the difference between good and evil. We choose forgiveness and repentance over hatred and retribution. To experience remorse for our actions or sorrow for those taken against us is indicative of the real work of the Holy Spirit within us. It is a sign of the abiding love that heals us.

What would have happened if the apostles and historians had just forgotten our Lord's crucifixion? What if Jesus had not inspired His story and purpose to be remembered through the Holy Scriptures? Would His suffering have meaning if walls were built around it so it could not be remembered? Could we make it through life—and what hope would we have if that were the case? Just as we remember His sacrifice for us in order to help us get over tough times, by remembering our own painful events, we can help others who might walk that same path. We can relate to them and their fears as no one else. We can be assured that we really have the abiding love of our Lord.

There are things that can hinder our ability to abide in God as well as His ability to abide in us, and they are all centered in desire. If we desire the things here more than the future spiritual life in Him, we will have a very difficult time truly uniting with the Holy Spirit. Our lives and actions will be self-serving and self-centered. No one can really abide in our Lord if he or she holds on to anything in this present age, whether it is anger, fear, hatred, unforgiveness, or unrepentance. The more we empty ourselves of these trappings of the adversary, the more our Lord can fill us with His love. The more we let go of anything that takes our focus off eternity with Him, the more freedom we will experience.

It takes a lot of energy and work to hold on to this world. If you really desire to experience God's abiding love in you, I encourage you to let go of all possessions, desire, family—*everything*. Thank Abba, our Father in heaven, for everything you have, and then release it. I'm not saying that we have to sell or give everything away. What I am saying is that we should not hold onto it. It is all fleeting! Our Lord's Word is eternal and will not pass away. His relationship with those who love Him and call Him by name will last forever.

Romans 6:5–11 tells us that if we really are believers and followers of our Lord, then we are crucified with Him. Perhaps you've heard that we are made new or are new creations when we totally accept our Lord as our Savior. This is because from the time of the fall in the Garden of Eden, the creation of man as God intended was distorted. We were once so perfect that even when we were completely naked, there was no imperfection. After the fall, even our nakedness was shameful. When a person really and truly accepts our Lord and is willing to go to the cross with Him, then all shame and guilt are gone. We are not just a new creation; at that point, we are a re-creation—even more than Adam and Eve were. Our new, eternal life in and with our Lord will be free even from the temptation of sin. The tree of knowledge will contain no evil, and the tree of life will be eternal. We will enjoy unending holiness and light together with our Lord. This could not happen apart from the cross.

The death that Jesus suffered for us was to complete the Father's plan. From the beginning, He knew the adversary and his followers schemed against man. He knew man could not stand against the adversary. Thus, He kept hidden from both man and the adversary the events that took place in heaven and on earth. The things that had to be determined the fate of all. The Father knows those who will and will not accept the grace offered through our Lord's sacrifice, but it is offered to all.

Accepting this grace does not guarantee an easy or wealthy life here on earth. It does, however, guarantee a life that is eternal and free of sin, temptation, or evil of any sort—a place where light is present because of our Lord's presence. He is the way, the truth, and the light. There is no darkness. Joy and peace abound in completeness. There are no needs or wants, because we will be united with the Father through our Lord.

We will have and experience all God the Almighty Creator can offer. There will be no darkness—only light with a new life in and through our Lord and Savior, Jesus.

Chapter Meditations

1. What do you think you need to do in order to be acceptable to the Holy Spirit?

2. Who is the abiding love? What do you think makes Him want to abide with us?

3. Is there anyone in your life whom you have not forgiven? Remember, if Jesus, the Son of God, was willing to do what He did for us in order to forgive us, what possible right do we have to hold on to our unforgiveness and hate?

4. What do you think would happen if you forgave?

5. Is there anyone in your life whom you know that you have harmed and have not asked for forgiveness?

6. If you ask someone to forgive you or contact someone and extend forgiveness and it is not accepted by them, is forgiveness a done deal anyway? Do you believe God would honor this in the spiritual realm?

7. What do you think would happen if you asked someone you wronged to forgive you? Can you trust God to lead the way?

8. Meditate for a few moments on our Lord's sacrifice for you. Look at Him on the cross. Can you fully realize what He suffered so you would not have to? Write Him a thank you note.

CHAPTER TEN

From Bondage to Freedom

To abide in our Lord—to release the controls and worries to Him—does not guarantee a life of wealth, serenity, or peace. Doing so, in fact, causes the opposite, because we focus on our Lord, thus the kingdom to come. Jesus said, "I came to cause division" (Luke 12:51). Well, He is not a troublemaker; He is a problem-solver. By choosing to abide in Him, we choose a much different way of living. We become separate from the world and therefore are often persecuted by it.

Which of the apostles did not suffer? By Jesus' birth, life, death, and resurrection, our Lord proved to Satan, his hordes, and the entire world that He was willing, trustworthy, loyal, and filled with love for His children. If we are His true children, we should be willing and even anxious to prove ourselves to Him. By our sacrifices great and small, we show our Lord and those outside the body of Christ that we are willing to follow Him no matter the cost. If we follow Him, we are on the road to our own Golgotha. But we are also on our own road to redemption—our own personal resurrection when our Lord will take us home. But before we are taken home, we can be united *in* Him in thought, word, and deed. Our lives are then directed from the spiritual realm but played out on a stage set here on earth.

By a true desire to be united in Him, we are called to be salt and light to the world. This cannot happen if we are apart from Him. Salt gives taste to food. We are to give taste and reason to life. Once we begin to abide in Him, all the troubles of this world become manageable. We begin to realize that the troubles of this world are temporary. They are not really a part us, and they do not define who we are. A beggar to the world is just that! We tend to judge him on the basis of his place in our hierarchy of economic status. To our Lord, he is another Lazarus. The begging does not define who he is *in* our Lord; it simply shows the possible results of choices made apart from our Lord. He is still a child of God! If the beggar were to repent and come to our Lord—to abide in Him—he may even remain a beggar, but his heart and mind would be united with Jesus. Jesus and the beggar would both rejoice every time someone put a quarter in his hand. I can see Jesus smiling and hugging the beggar, spinning him around as He shouts, "Look what that person gave us!"

To abide in our Lord, we must have our hearts and minds clear and open to Him and Him alone, free of the cares and worries of the world, because we have placed them in His hands. If we are still holding on to the junk in our lives, it would be like inviting Him to our home and having the living room so cluttered that there is no place for Him to sit and rest. These are not easy lessons, and some need time to become teachable. We must come to a place in our lives where we make the real, final choice to unite with Him. In order to do this, we must realize that our free will is actually given to us so that we can freely and willingly give it back to God. We do this by relinquishing all that we have on this earth to Him who gave it to us. We allow Him to unite His perfect will with ours and return it to us. From that point on, whether we are beggars or presidents, we live for Him and His glory. For some of us, this is difficult—and I was no exception.

In 1998, Doni and I moved to Southern California, and my mind and heart were far from ready for God. I had certainly not released my will to Him. It is surprising to me how often we can step out to serve Him or minister in His name when we do not really know Him. It is only by His grace that any of this could succeed.

When we settled in California, Doni's sister, Rhonda, invited us to a fairly new church in Costa Mesa called Rock Harbor. Although it was new, it had grown rapidly, and the average weekly attendance was about eight hundred. Doni and I were asked to be a part of a church committee that researched the probability of implementing a cell church model as a foundational system at Rock Harbor. For various reasons, the leaders of Rock Harbor chose to maintain a small group paradigm but abandoned the actual cell church concept. Although this was our initial involvement with Rock Harbor, it simply set the stage for God's plan to bring us individual and marital healing.

At this time, our marriage was suffering from blows and beatings of the adversary. These were brought on mostly by our own selfish desires and the fact we were not even remotely focused on God's will for us. Of course, everyone knows marriage issues are always the other person's fault, and our marriage was no different. I was after all a wonderful husband and a exemplary man! One morning, after my wife and I had spent another night on opposite sides of the bed, I walked into the living room and said, "If we are going to get a divorce, let's do it now so I can be on my motorcycle and in Florida before the snows hit the Midwest." Great guy, huh? Our eyes were so focused on each other's faults that we could not see the outstretched hand that our Lord extended toward us. We were in serious trouble, but God had a plan.

One morning after the church service, I felt a strong urge to talk to the pastor. I had noticed there was no pastoral care ministry at Rock Harbor. I told the pastor my master's degree was in this field and that I would help him set it up, but I did not want to have any other involvement. What I did not know was that the staff had prayed for our Lord to send someone for this needed ministry. Within a short time, I found myself with the position of Pastoral Care Minister. Doni became head of the prayer team, which met every Monday to pray over the many requests from the previous day. These two ministries were very intense, and they helped us take our eyes off ourselves long enough for God to soften our hearts and open our eyes to Him.

About three months after we began these ministries, we received a phone call from the church office. The secretary asked us if we could attend a seminar in Van Nuys, California. I asked what the seminar was about, and she told me she was not sure. I think she actually lied (but in Christian love). I was told later that no one else in the office had the courage to go, and someone said, "Ask the Trenkle's; they are up for about anything."

As it turned out, the seminar was at the Church on the Way in Van Nuys. The Pastor, Jack Hayford, was the seminar facilitator for the entire weekend. This was to be a life-changing event! This was the first time either Doni or I had ever been introduced to spiritual warfare. We were gifted with an entire weekend of teaching from a man whose life is totally led by the Holy Spirit of God. During this weekend, we learned about the demonic realm and the many ways we leave ourselves open to attacks. We also learned about generational curses and how they can have an effect on many areas of our lives. Most importantly, we began to learn how to protect ourselves from these attacks by taking an offensive stand against the enemy instead of a defensive stand. Pastor Hayford offered a second weekend seminar entitled "Cleansing Stream" that Doni and I both attended. By the time the second weekend was over, we both fully realized the bondage we lived under and knew that we needed to do something about it. We desperately wanted to live our lives as Pastor Hayford had described—free from oppression and in union with our Lord.

Shortly after the second seminar, Doni urged a girlfriend of hers to help her walk through a deliverance ministry. A very dear friend of mine actually paid the expenses to fly a couple to Costa Mesa and minister deliverance to me. I know many people take exception to using the word *deliverance* when it comes to believers, but I was delivered! Demons had to leave, ordered out by the name above all names—Jesus. Doni and I have walked in freedom since that time. This has not been an easy road, but life on this planet will never be easy!

One of the most amazing things is what transpired over the next year. People began inviting me to attend seminars with them. These seminars were based on spiritual warfare and deliverance ministry. We had people come to us at church and say, "I don't know why, but I was supposed to give you this book." The books were always about deliverance and spiritual warfare.

At that time, Doni and I managed an apartment building in Costa Mesa. Because I had once been a police officer, our personal phone was an unlisted number, yet we began getting phone calls for ministry from church hotlines throughout Southern California. For almost a year, we ministered deliverance to at least two people each day. It was exciting and rewarding for us to witness people set free from the bondage they had been held in for years.

I will have to say the fire of this excitement is quickly dampened when we witness people return to the bondage that once held them captive. Why would a person who was set free by our Lord go back to the old way of life? I believe they do this because it's the only life they have ever known, and they can't *control* their new environment. That is exactly the issue! Instead of giving the controls to Jesus and uniting with His will, we fight to maintain control over ourselves. Perhaps someone convinced these people that their experience was not real. In any event, the truth is that without seeking freedom from the workings of the demonic realm, living a life completely *in* our Lord, and having Him in us, is almost impossible. The Holy Spirit will never be free to work through us if the chains of the past hold us captive.

If we can learn what it means to be in Christ, life becomes easier to handle. We will all have difficulties in life whether we believe in our Lord or not. God has an enemy, and as His children, so do we. Even people who do not believe in our Lord are assaulted by the adversary. Instead of recognizing the real source of the calamities, they blame such things on karma or bad luck. This makes the demonic realm very happy. The focus is on a non-tangible entity, so the person does not even try to resist the enemy. Our Lord said, "Resist the devil and he will flee." (James 4:7) If we do not recognize the root to the present evil in our lives, we will not resist. We will not fight!

For a believer who has been set free from the bondage of past sin, two things should become evident. First, that person should be very aware when the enemy attacks. He should be able to defend himself rather than falling into the snare that was set. We should become cognizant of our primary weaknesses—the areas of bondage through which our flesh is most susceptible. The second thing that becomes evident is that we are called to be on the offensive, not on the defensive. When we abide *in* our Lord and truly have His Holy Spirit in us, demons should flee when we enter a room. We should never wait to be attacked or make the statement that we are expecting attacks. We should awaken every morning with excitement that we are going to do the work of God, remembering the promises of our Lord. By the power of His name, the powers of darkness will not stand against us.

> We should awaken every morning with excitement that we are going to do the work of God

We are all called to be warriors for Christ. I will fight, and I will not give in—not just to be free from the flaming darts of the enemy, but also to be free of all the things that may inhibit my relationship with God. It's fulfilling to be free in spirit to worship my Lord and experience the joy of the Lord. None of this comes easily, and it does not come without a battle or two.

Chapter Meditation

1. What is your primary area of bondage by which the adversary holds you enslaved?

2. Are you willing to give this bondage up?

3. What sacrifices would you be willing to accept as a part of the body of our Lord?

4. How are you salt and light to the world around you?

5. What does "Resist the devil" mean to you, and how can you do this?

CHAPTER ELEVEN

We Preach Better Sermons with Our Lives than with Our Lips

As I reread this chapter, I had a feeling readers would close the book here and not complete it. I went to our Lord and said, "Lord, this chapter just does not seem exciting."

God's response was, "Joel, that is what most people feel about following me and living a life in My will. It is not about the excitement of life; it is about the joy found in it and in Me."_So I invite you to enjoy this chapter as we explore together how to live a life in joy and in Jesus.

In order to love as Jesus loves, we must forgive as He did. He suffered and died so that we could be reunited with the Father. The Father longs for us. His love for us is far greater than the Devil's hatred. He really wants us to be a part of Him even while we are on earth. Father God came and walked in the garden with our ancestors, Adam and Eve. He gave Adam and Eve everything, and He trusted them. They betrayed that trust, just as you and I have on occasion through our own sin against Him. Even then, He did not turn away. He sent His only Son to redeem that sin—to ransom us back. What He asks in return is that we are obedient and show our love for Him, as He demonstrates His love for us by forgiving all of our wrongdoings. Then we can experience and demonstrate to others the joy of the Father as it is lived out in us.

We can be joyful in all matters. This does not mean we will necessarily be happy about our situation, since there is a difference. James 1:2–4 tells us, "Regard it all as joy, my brothers, when you face various kinds of temptations; for you know that the testing of your trust produces perseverance. But let perseverance do its complete work; so that you may be complete and whole, lacking nothing." This is a hard statement for most of us to swallow, especially if we are in the middle of one of those life-and-death situations, but we can learn to live in the peace of God, which surpasses all human understanding.

As we observe in Scripture, all people were created with two things in common. First, everyone was given free will—the ability to make decisions in life for ourselves. Second, we were all created in the likeness and image of the Father, God (Genesis 1:26, 5:1). It is only by exercising this free will that we can truly be *in* Jesus. When a person is baptized into the faith, he or she makes a statement of belief in our Lord as the Messiah—that the birth, life, death on the cross, and resurrection of Jesus atoned for our sins and opened the gates of heaven to us. Baptism is an outward sign that He releases his will to our Lord. Then Jesus can return that gift offered to Him along with His own gift—*His will* for that person, which once united with the person's will; the two become one.

If a person is a true believer—if he or she was baptized as a public display of love and belief in our Lord—the Father will send the Spirit, the *Ruach HaKodesh* (Holy Spirit), to unite him or her forever with God (John 14:26; John 20:22; Acts 1:5; Acts 8:14-15). The Holy Spirit can only enter a willing vessel. The Spirit brings His giftedness to that person. The entire process is an outward sign—a profession to the people on the earth as well as to the spirit realm that he or she chose to join with God and be united in Him. It is expected that each person who is baptized will use the gifts given by the Father to further His kingdom while on earth.

The gifts of the Holy Spirit are listed in 1 Corinthians 12. Beginning with verse 4, Paul tells us,

> Now there are different kinds of gifts, but the same Spirit gives them. Also there are different ways of serving, but it is the same Lord being served. And there are different modes of working, but it is the same God working them all in everyone. We can observe the triune God working in us all for the common good. Moreover, to each person is given the particular manifestation of the Spirit that will be for the common good. To one, through the Spirit, is given a word of wisdom; to another, a word of knowledge, in accordance with the same Spirit; to another faith by the same Spirit; and to another, gifts of healing, by that one Spirit; to another, the working of miracles; to another, prophecy; to another, the ability to judge between spirits; to another, the ability to speak in different kinds of tongues; and to yet another, the ability to interpret tongues. One and the same Spirit is at work in all these things, distributing to each person as he chooses. For just as the body is one that has many parts; and all the parts of the body, though many, constitute one body; so it is with the Messiah. For it was by one Spirit that we were all immersed into one body, whether Jews or Gentiles, slaves or free; and we were all given the one Spirit to drink.

Notice the unity both with God and each other! There is no class distinction; we are all one and the same. We are to prayerfully discover what gifts of the Spirit we were given and then use those gifts *for the sole purpose of glorifying God* by ministering to the body of Jesus on this earth. If we willingly receive baptism, we join the kingdom of the Father. Why wouldn't we want to work for the kingdom, since we now belong to it?

Baptism into the body of our Lord is not a hedge fund. It is not a get-out-of-jail-free card. Unless it is taken seriously and for the purpose of being united with God, it is really a meaningless bath. A person should seriously consider this to be a life-altering decision. Additionally, unity with God does not necessarily guarantee us an easy life. In Matthew 7:13, Jesus stated, "Go in through the narrow gate; for <u>the gate that leads to destruction</u> is wide and the road broad, and many travel it; but it is a narrow gate and a hard road that leads to life, and only a few find it."

In Matthew 7:21, our Lord stated, "Not everyone who says to me, 'Lord, Lord!' will enter into the Kingdom of Heaven, only those who do what my Father in heaven wants. On that day many will say to me, 'Lord, Lord! Didn't we prophesy in your name? Didn't we expel demons in your name? Didn't we perform many miracles in your name?' Then I will tell them to their faces, 'I never knew you! Get away from me, you workers of lawlessness!'" You see, we do not join a club; we unite ourselves with God the Almighty Father. This is serious stuff! If we do not have a personal relationship with our Lord and truly *know Him,* then we live a lie, and the truth is not in us.

When a true believer seeks and receives the gifts of the Holy Spirit after baptism, he or she actually receives the *tools* God intends him or her to use. We are to use these gifts in order to till the soil and help produce a harvest of souls who will enjoy the eternal kingdom with God.

The evidence that our membership is real and our motives are pure is demonstrated by the fruit we bear for God. Galatians 5:22–23 explains that the fruit of the Spirit is love, joy, peace, patience, kindness, goodness, faithfulness, humility, and self-control. In Galatians 5:24, Paul explained, "Those who belong to the Messiah Yeshua (Jesus) have put their old nature to death on the stake, along with its passions and desires. Since it is through the Spirit that we have life, let it also be through the Spirit that we order our lives day by day." Here again, we can plainly see that a person releases his or her will to the Father. He or she is baptized in water and the Spirit as an outward sign that he or she has died to the self and been raised in union with Jesus to the service of God. That person's life is forever changed. The evidence of that change becomes obvious by the fruit that person begins to bear.

If we are in our Lord and He is in us, through the power of the Holy Spirit, we become patient, as He is patient. We will love as He loves. We will possess and demonstrate peace, kindness, joy, goodness, faithfulness, humility, and self-control.

The peace of the Father is one of the most evident truths of the Holy Spirit. *Shalom,* the peace of God is only found in a true believer. Men and women who do not live lives in our Lord may demonstrate a sort of peace, but it is not eternal peace. It will not last. God's peace is peace found through an acceptance of existence on earth. Real *shalom* is found through acceptance of and belief in a totally intangible entity. It is found in a person's faith. That faith leads to belief and an understanding of the true will of the Father. It leads to union with God, not oneness with the universe.

Shalom is only obtained through the power of the Holy Spirit. It is found in a willingness to surrender the things of this world in order to be united, even now, with the eternal kingdom. Nothing we have here will remain. It will all be destroyed on the day of our Lord (Joel 2:1–2, Isaiah 24:3–6, Matthew 24:21). *Shalom* gives the believer the ability to inwardly endure hardships, just as our Lord did, while outwardly working to advance the kingdom of the Father on earth. It was through the power of this *shalom* that our Lord could carry His cross. It was through *shalom* that He was able to hang on that cross for us. Due to that inner peace, Jesus was able to demonstrate and live a life of patience.

Patience is really endurance. It is evidence that the gifts of the Father are present in us and that God is working through us. Life can seem like a pointless battleground, and without patient endurance, we might not finish the race. This world will not last, because it has become part of the corruption of the adversary; thus it is in constant turmoil, and everyone here must endure it. Through patience found in the Spirit of

God, the new kingdom will be advanced and prepared while we are on earth. Patience in times of trouble and even disasters will be noticed by all. Believers will understand when a person remains calm in the midst of a storm, because they are in union with the Almighty Creator, God. The unbeliever will marvel at and envy the courage and stamina of the believer, much as Emperor Nero did as he watched the early Christian martyrs singing songs of praise as they entered the arena to be killed.

Do you think Paul might have marveled at St. Steven's courage as he was stoned to death? (Acts 7:55–60, 8:1) Steven's death is an example of how *Jesus works all things for the glory of the Father.* If we stop to absorb this statement, we realize that everything that happens has or will have a miracle attached to it. Steven's death led the way to the gentile nations coming to the faith. After his death, believers who feared they, too, would be killed were scattered throughout the known world. Because these believers received the Holy Spirit, they did not lose faith in this dispersion but shared the Word of God and new way of life. Steven's death led the way to the gentile nations. After Paul (Sha"ul) accepted our Lord and came to believe that Yeshua was the long-awaited Messiah, he was also united in the Lord Jesus by the work and power of the Holy Spirit. He willingly devoted the rest of his life as a witness to the truth found only in the union with the Messiah—Jesus, our Lord.

Looking back on my life, I can readily observe blessings behind every hardship. Patient endurance will, in most cases, help us to see these blessings—but not always. The fact that Paul was able to bring the good news of salvation to the gentiles and the world is evident today, but it was not anticipated by Paul and those who followed the way in the first century. We must take some things on faith, for we know that in all things, God works for the good of those who love Him—who have been called according to His purpose and pleasure (Romans 8:28). As we wait upon the Lord, we cannot live life in Him without being patient and kind to others. Kindness is also evidence or fruit of the Spirit that demonstrates that we are united in our Lord and that He resides in us.

Kindness is *compassion* and care for others. All the spiritual tools needed for work are found in kindness. It leads us to want to bring physical comfort and spiritual wholeness to those who are lost and hurting. Through kindness, a person's eyes are opened to the work of the Father.

If we are in the Lord and He is in us, goodness becomes second nature to us. It becomes a desire! We want to be good and do good deeds—not for our own notoriety, but because through those acts, the goodness shown to others increases the joy we feel within. We are joyful, because the Holy Spirit within us is pleased. Once a person actually experiences the joy of the Lord, he or she cannot be satisfied with any other pleasure. This union within us is as close as a mortal being can be to the eternal. It prepares us to enter the eternal kingdom. The fruits of the most Holy Spirit all work together to bring fullness and purpose to life. If people do not live in union with the Lord, what purpose is there for their lives? Why would a real believer seek to do anything else? We either live to serve God or to satisfy and serve the self. We cannot do both.

If we live to be in union with the Lord and to serve Almighty God, we will obtain faithfulness. We will become filled with the pleasure of doing God's will. We can be trusted by the Father. Faithfulness is a virtue of the Almighty God. All the fruits are aspects of the very makeup of the Father. He is faithful, and He knows those who live in the freedom granted to all through the redemption paid by our Lord on the cross. These are people who can be trusted by God to do His work.

When the Father recognizes that a person's heart is really joined in union with our Lord, He can give that person the power of the Holy Spirit. By the authority given in the name of Jesus, the signs and wonders of the Spirit of God are accomplished on earth. In the gospel of John 14:12, Jesus told Philip, "Yes, indeed! I tell you that whoever trusts in Me will also do the works I do! Indeed, he will do greater ones, because I am going to the Father. In fact, whatever you ask in my name I will do; so that the Father may be glorified in the Son. If you ask Me for something in my name, I will do it."

When the miraculous occurs through a believer, an explosive thing happens! In the spiritual realm, the adversary knows that the flow of God's redemptive work has moved from heaven to earth. On earth, people see the results and wait for a moment to observe what the witness to the event will say. If the believer takes the credit, he or she is done! If, however, he or she gives God the glory, honor is bestowed upon him or her in the heavenly realm. The Father bestows humility upon us for our faithfulness and willingness to be trustworthy in these great matters.

A true miracle worker knows full well the power moving through him or her and its origin. This person can't help but become humbled in the face of the power of God shown through the Holy Spirit. We are to seek the Father's will and to be united with the Father through our union with Jesus. Jesus said all things would be granted when a person asks in his name, but whatever we ask, must bring glory to the Father. (John 15:16) The believer who is really united with the Lord must seek first the will of the Father in every situation; then do as he hears and sees the Father doing. We are commanded to first seek the kingdom of God and its righteousness. This is the exercise of self-control in union with the Holy Spirit of God the Father.

Chapter Meditations

1. What does baptism mean to you? Has your view changed in any way?

2. Has this chapter changed your picture of who a true believer in our Lord is?

3. What gifts do you feel the Holy Spirit has given you? How do or will you use them?

4. Do you believe that you are worthy to receive and use these gifts? Why or why not?

5. Have you done anything that you feel the death of the Son of God on the cross could not atone for? If so, ask Yeshua (Jesus) right now to forgive you; then listen with your heart for His reply.

CHAPTER TWELVE

A New Life in Our Final Days

Pastor Jack Hayford, pastor of Church on the Way in Van Neyes, California, once stated, "It does not really matter if you are pre-tribulation or post-tribulation; if you are alive, you are in your last days." These are difficult times. It is hard not to get caught up in the evil politics of the world. Man was created in the likeness and image of God. Most have a natural desire to make crooked paths straight, but in these times, that is simply not often possible.

Evil people are taking the world by storm. Every nation, including the United States, has moved away from the principles of God. Some Christian denominations have endeavored to twist the Scriptures to accommodate their own divisiveness and to justify their separation from the truths found in the Scriptures. Their attempts to become politically correct and to coexist lead many to live lifestyles of sin that will ultimately bring them judgment by our Lord. Jesus does not desire to judge us when we leave this place. He desires to greet us with a kiss and tell us, "Well done, good and faithful servant!" He has gone the extra measure to give us this opportunity to abide in Him both now and for eternity.

I have attempted to direct us to a place of abiding and peace found only in the Savior. Problematically, whenever we are presented with any opportunity, it seems that the first question is, "What's in it for me?" This abiding in Jesus is not exactly easy. We are swimming upstream against the world's views. So what do we achieve by abiding in our Lord? This is the question I had to answer and that you must also answer. Developing a lifestyle leading to abiding in our Lord is an individual aspiration, but we still have to live in a world that is becoming completely corrupt.

We can run after earthly wealth, pleasure, and honor and receive an earthly prize that will not last. However, if we seek our Lord, we receive rewards that last into eternity. How do I know this to be true? Is it just because I read a collection of writings in a book? No! It is because only Yeshua—Jesus, the Son of God—could accomplish what He did on earth, as it is in heaven, in order to open the door to eternal life for us. Some scholars claim that before, during, and after His lifetime, He fulfilled over 340 prophecies from the *Tanakh* (Old Testament). A mere man has no control over where, how, and to whom he is born. Yet this man, the Son of God, had everything to do with the completion of the Father's plan.

His birth was foretold by the prophet Isaiah nearly 700 years prior to His conception. In Isaiah 7:14, the prophet stated, "Therefore Adonai Himself will give us a sign; a young woman will become pregnant, bear a son and name him Immanuel El (God is with us)." The Hebrew word *almah* in Isaiah 7:14 refers to a young woman. In the context of the *Tanakh,* it always refers to a young woman of unsullied reputation, which is why the Jewish translators of the Septuagint (the Greek version of the *Tanakh*), prepared over two hundred years before the birth of Yeshua, renders this word into the Greek as *parthenos,* which means "virgin." This word is also used in Matthew 1:23.[1] Micah 5:1–2 said that He would be born in *Biet-Lechem,* in *Y'huda* (Bethlehem in Judah). The fact that He would be a descendant of David and heir to his throne is found in 2 Samuel 7:12–13, Isaiah 9:6–7, and Jeremiah 23:5. Even the slaughter of the children in Bethlehem after His birth by King Herod was prophesied in Jeremiah 31:15 and described in Matthew 2:18. Rabbi

Glenn Blank of *Biet Simcha* Messianic Fellowship once stated, "God is unknowable unless He shows Himself to us to eliminate the barrier between us. The Bible told us how He would do this; that He would come into the world as a human being."

Besides the virgin birth, other prophecies in Isaiah which were also fulfilled include: He would be called Son of God, Isaiah 9:6-7; A messenger would precede Him (John the Baptizer) Isaiah 40:1-5; God's salvation would reach to the ends of the earth, Isaiah 49:6; Yeshua would be spat upon and beaten, Isaiah 50:6; He would be rejected, Isaiah 53:1-3; He would die for our sins, Isaiah 53:4-6; He would be silent before His accusers, 53:7; He would be buried in a rich man's tomb, Isaiah 53:9.

It is obvious that Yeshua was not an ordinary man. He was and is the anticipated Messiah. He is the completion of God's promise to the Jews who are His chosen people. *The Jew who comes to understand this and accepts Yeshua as Messiah remains a Jew. He is not a Christian! He is a completed Jew; awaiting the promises of an eternal inheritance we all are given.* Those of us who were not born Jewish and accepted Jesus as the Messiah are grafted into this rich Jewish lineage. By accepting Jesus, we are adopted by this chosen race of people. We are spiritually united with our Jewish brothers and sisters God chose thousands of years ago as His own. He led them out of bondage to the Babylonians and Egyptians and resurrected them from the ashes of the Holocaust. It is His desire to lead us as a shepherd out of the bondage of this world. To abide in Him—to follow this shepherd who has already proven His love and desire to protect us from the adversary—is to enjoy *shalom*. This peace surpasses all understanding, because it is supernatural.

By willingly abiding in Jesus, we will be able to leave the cares of this world behind us and direct our lives toward the future with Him. By uniting with Him, we can live life with the unity of the Holy Spirit of God. Once we experience the overflow of love from the Holy Spirit that dwells within us and the joy of being in the presence of our Lord Jesus, the things of the earth no longer seem necessary. By abiding in our Lord, we seek and eventually receive the true nature of the Father. By becoming holy, as our Lord Jesus is holy, we earn the right to be called sons and daughters of God. It is our birthright because of our call from the Holy Spirit.

> What is the peace that surpasses all understanding? It is the ability to live in and endure the hard times and day-to-day issues of this fallen state of being, because we feel the flow of eternal life within our spirits.

Jesus died for everyone—but only those whose hearts *can* be turned and united with Christ will be called by the Holy Spirit. There are many whom the Spirit knows will not turn and submit to the Father. They will not unite their will with His. They will never be united with the Triune God. This fact saddens me greatly, and it also grieves the Lord. But *you cannot force anyone to love Jesus. You cannot force anyone to quit loving himself or herself.* People who seek only the pleasures of the world love only themselves.

If we learn to be content with what we are given, we demonstrate that we are thankful, submissive, and humble. When the Father blesses us by satisfying our needs, we recognize these blessings as gifts, not something deserved, and we will rejoice. It is a blessing or grace the Father bestows upon us.

There is a definition for the word *grace* that I use often: Grace is the receipt of an undeserved reward when our actions and thoughts really earned us a penalty of death. We receive grace when we receive our Lord Jesus. We receive Him when nothing else matters. Once we receive Him—when we are in Him and He is in us—His peace (His *shalom*) can flow through our spiritual veins and nourish our souls and spirits. What is the peace that surpasses all understanding? It is the ability to live in and endure the hard times and day-to-day issues of this fallen state of being, because we feel the flow of eternal life within our spirits. Remember, we are in this world but not of it.

Have you ever traveled to a foreign land, or visited a different city or state? Do you remember the sights, smells of the marketplaces, and differences in dress and culture of the people? I vividly recall sitting on a patio of a restaurant in Vung Tau, Vietnam. This patio was constructed so that it hung on the edge of the building, protruding over the ocean. The waves broke against the rocks below, and the salt water spray misted us and cooled us from the heat of the day. I remember brushing the flies away from my water buffalo steak as I relaxed over my meal.

As you might imagine, I knew that Vietnam was not home. I did not really belong, and I knew I would eventually return to my real home. This is what an abiding life in Jesus is like. We are here, but we know in our hearts that we do not really belong. What is required? We must stop worrying! We are to cease striving and know that He is God. He will take care of our every need.

Do you recall the beggar in the previous chapter? Begging was not all he could do. Because he found a treasure abiding in our Lord, his state in this life seemed meaningless. His eyes were focused on eternity. His spirit could feel the fullness of his union with Jesus. Relaxing in the arms of our Lord when we are weary or troubled, letting Him hold us and rock us to sleep, dancing with Him, rejoicing when we know we are in His presence, and feeling our spirits calm to the point of being overjoyed and joyful tears flow uncontrollably— this is what abiding in our Lord can be. It is experiencing what life can really become.

When we accept Jesus and abide in Him, the chains of the sin of Adam and Eve are broken. When we abide in Him, we open the door and place a foot on the threshold of eternal life. Finishing the race here is simply the start of our eternal service to the Father. The door to the kingdom is never locked, because only those who are willing to walk the narrow road arrive. The door is theirs to open.

<u>Final Meditation</u>

If you will choose to abide in God—to AIM for Him—tell Him so. Write a covenant here between you and Yeshua, and date it. Then finish with a personal love letter to the wonderful, gentle shepherd who lay down and died so that we could live.

ABOUT THE AUTHORS

Joel and Doni Trenkle

Joel received his bachelor's degree in majors in Religious Studies and Psychology from Regis University in 1983. He then completed his master's degree in Pastoral Care and Counseling from St. Thomas Seminary in 1984. He received his Doctor of Christian Ministry Degree from Christian Leadership University. Joel is a US Army Ranger and Vietnam combat veteran with extensive life experiences, which the Lord uses in conjunction with Joel's formal education to enable him to help others deal with the painful struggles we face in our daily lives.

Doni is co-author of *AIM—Abide in Me*. She has a bachelor's degree in Christian Ministry from Christian Leadership University Seminary. She is a strong prayer warrior and excellent pastoral counselor with a compassionate heart for all of God's people. Doni specializes in caring for women who have been victims of sexual trauma.

ENDNOTES

INTRODUCTION

1. Charles R. Swindoll, John F. Walvoord, J. Dwight Pentecost, *et al., The Road to Armageddon* (Nashville: Word Publishing, (1999), 6–7.

2. Stephen R. Covey, *The 7 Habits of Highly Effective Families* (New York: Golden Books, 1977).

3. *The Hoy Bible: New International Version* (Grand Rapids: Zondervan, 1984), Mark 16:15.

CHAPTER 3

1. Sarah Young, *Jesus Calling* (Nashville, Tennessee, Thomas Nelson, 2004).

2. David H. Stern, *Complete Jewish Bible* (Clarksville, Maryland: Jewish New Testament Publications, Inc., 1998).

CHAPTER 7

1. The word *Trinity* (Triune) does not appear in Scripture, but evidence is provided by our Lord.

Matthew 28:16–20: Matthew did not record the meeting of Jesus with the ten disciples later that same day (John 20:19–23) or the appearance eight days later to the eleven disciples (John 20:24–29). But he did record an appearance occurring some time later in Galilee, where Jesus promised He would meet them (Matthew 26:32, [1]cf. 28:7, 10) at a mountain. Which mountain He specified is unknown. When Jesus appeared, they worshiped Him, but some doubted. Since Jesus had appeared to them earlier and verified Himself to them, they did not doubt the resurrection. There was probably a brief question among some of them as to whether Jesus truly appeared to them. There was no indication that any miraculous element was involved in His being there; since unusual circumstances had occurred with previous visits, perhaps they wondered.

Their doubts were quickly dispelled, for Jesus spoke to them, claiming all authority in heaven and on earth. This authority (*exousia*, "official right or power") was given to Jesus by the Father. Jesus instructed the disciples to go on the basis of that authority. Their field was to include all nations, not just Israel (Matthew 28:19; Mark 16:15; Luke 24:47) They were to make disciples by proclaiming the truth concerning Jesus. Their hearers were to be evangelized and enlisted as Jesus' followers.

Those who believed were to be baptized in water in the name of the Father, Son, and Holy Spirit. Such an act would associate a believer with the person of Jesus Christ and the Triune God. The God they served is one God and yet three persons—Father, Son, and Holy Spirit. Those who respond are also to be taught the truths Jesus specifically communicated to the eleven. Not all that Jesus taught the disciples was communicated by them, but they did teach specific truths for the new church age as they went abroad. Jesus' commission, applicable to all His followers, involved one command: "Make disciples." This is accompanied by three participles in the Greek: going, baptizing, and teaching.

---

1   cf. *confer*, compare

CHAPTER 8

1. *Tom Tiede, Albuquerque Tribune,* April 18, 1966.

CHAPTER 11

1. David H. Stern, *Complete Jewish Bible* (Clarksville, Maryland: Jewish New Testament Publications, Inc., 1998).

SCRIPTURE INDEX

Chapter 1

Mark 16:15, Matthew 24:9, John 16:33, Acts 9:16, John 14:6

Chapter 2

Matthew 16:22–23, James 4:4, Matthew 15:18–19

Chapter 3

Matthew 15:27; 1 John 3:1; Romans 1:17; Jeremiah 29:11; Luke 10:38–42; Matthew 25:1, 5–6, 10; Mark 2:19–20; Luke 5:34–35; John 2:9, 3:29; Romans 5:8

Chapter 4

Psalm 141:8; Revelation 2:1–4; John 14:6; John 11:25–26; John 8:28–29, 14:3, 12

Chapter 5

James 2:11

Chapter 6

Matthew 12:36, James 1:26–30, James 3:4–12

Chapter 7

Romans 5:8, 6:1, 13, 17; 2 Corinthians 10:4–5; 1 Corinthians 13:4–5; Jeremiah 1:5; Psalm 139:13–14; Luke 15:7

Chapter 8

1 Corinthians 4:9–13

Chapter 9
Matthew 15:18–19; Romans 6:5–11

Chapter 10
Luke 12:51

Chapter 11
James 1:2–4; Genesis 1:26, 5:1; John 14:12, 26, 20:22; Acts 1:5, 8; 1 Corinthians 12:4–13; Matthew 7:13, 21, 24:21; Galatians 5:22–23; Joel 2:1–2; Isaiah 24:3–6; Acts 7:55–60, 8:1

Chapter 12
Isaiah 9:6–7, 7:14; Matthew 1:23, 2:18; Micah 5:1–2; 2 Samuel 7:12–13; Jeremiah 23:5, 31:15

INDEX

fruit of the Spirit 88, 90

G

grace is the receiving of an undeserved reward when our actions and thoughts really earned us a penalty of death. 98
guilt, 42

H

Hananyah 4
healing ii, 22, 63, 71, 79, 87
Holy Spirit ix, 11, 12, 37, 62, 63, 67, 72, 74, 80, 81, 82, 86, 88, 89, 90, 91, 92, 93, 97, 98, 104

I

'I never knew you 88

J

Jack Hayford 95
joy 36, 43, 53, 59, 85, 86, 88, 89, 91, 97, 99

K

knowledge of total good 35

L

Learning 8
learning challenges 18
life of wealth 77
lifestyle 17
lifestyle of 'abiding' 20

M

Monsignor O'Sullivan 18
motives 88

N

North Vietnamese 56
NVA 56

O

our primary weaknesses 82

P

parents 2, 3, 29, 42, 43, 44
Pastoral Care 79
Pastor, Jack Hayford 80
pattern of life 50
pattern of teaching 50, 51
personal view 18
politically correct 95
prepared over 200 years before the birth of Yeshua 96
Prophet Isaiah 96
pure and holy 49
Purple Hearts 69

R

real truth 29
red ants 27
relationship 17
righteous 1, 2, 20, 53
Rock Harbor 79
Ruach HaKodesh 86

S

Salt 78
Samuel 59
Sarah Young 25
second eternal death 11
serenity 77
Shalom, 89
shame 42
Sha'ul 4
Sister Mary Elvadine 18
Soldiers do not return to their loved ones as they left them. They leave parts of themselves on the battle-fields, and carry with them the memories of what was, and the dreams of what might have been. 69
spiritual footprint 68

St.Vincent DePaul 20, 44
Swindoll, Charles R. 1

T

taking an offensive stand 30, 80
Tanakh 96
the enemy intended for evil 44
the heart 13, 62, 67
the Iron Triangle 56
the more we have, the harder we will
       have to work to keep it. 30

U

ultimate healer 71
unconditional love 49, 60, 67
unforgiveness 42
united in 77

V

Van Nuys 80
Viet Nam 56
voice ii, ix, xi, 18, 35, 57, 58

W

We're supposed to stand out, not to fit
       in! 28
Whamo 55
wounded people 42

Y

yoke 7
You do not have to love a person to
       forgive them\; you need to love
       our Lord! 68

CPSIA information can be obtained
at www.ICGtesting.com
Printed in the USA
FSOW02n1030041214
3702FS